To Lilia)

Felix

The
Pebble
and the
Canyon

Reflections on Composing Your Life

Felix M. Scardino

Shining Brightly Books
Houston, Texas
2008

Shining Brightly Books
11010 Hanning Lane
Houston, Texas 770041
Fax — 713-896-9887   rita.mills@yahoo.com

www.PebbleandtheCanyon.com

Scardino, Felix M.: 1937 -
     The pebble and the canyon : reflections on composing your life /
Felix M. Scardino.
     p. cm.
     ISBN -- 978-0-9800061-5-5
1. Self-actualization (Psychology). 2. Self-help techniques. 3. Conduct of life. 4. Creative Solutions. I. Title.

BF637.S4 S3 2007
153.3222—dc22   2007939456

Production Team
Rita Mills of The Book Connection — Project Manager
www.bookconnectiononline.com
Peggy Stautberg & Deborah Frontiera — Conceptual Editing
Faye Walker — Line Editing
Galdys Ramirez — Cover Design   Author Portrait — Larry Flake

The paper used in this publication meets the requirements of the American National Standard for Permanence of Paper for Printed Library Materials Z39.48-1984.

Printed in the United States of America

Contents

To my wife,

Patsy

Acknowledgments

I f I thanked every person whose counsel, support, and encouragement kept me afloat while writing this book, the list would be far too long. However, I would be remiss without making the following acknowledgments.

Thanks to the countless clients whose lives of determination and openness I have been privileged to witness. Mostly this book chronicles their struggles, growth, and renewal.

Thanks to Marcia Chamberlain, my writing coach, for pointing the way to simplicity, integrity, and consistency in writing. A master blend of diplomacy and directness, Marcia can say gently and kindly, "This sentence stinks."

Thanks to Joyce James, my writing teacher. With jitters and trepidation, I joined her class at the Houston Community College shortly after I decided to write this book. At that time, I was still wondering if I could write. From Joyce I heard that I could.

Thanks to my writing group of some years ago, including Suzan Cotellesse, Richard Stork, Lucia Bettler, and Gene Webb, for their support and helpful criticism.

Thanks to Mary Jo Piwetz, Candace Jones, and Shannon Holloway for being a test-lab for a key exercise in the book.

Thanks to Bill Stott, Professor Emeritus of American Studies and English, at The University of Texas at Austin, for reading the rough draft of the book and suggesting how to bring it to life. Also, thanks to Bill for writing *Write to the Point, and Feel Better about Your Writing*, a book of enormous influence on my decision to write.

Thanks to JoAnn Butera, Michael Bettler, Joanna Matranga, and Lynn Murphy for reading the almost-final manuscript and giving me helpful feedback.

Thanks to Beth Allen for her work and advice toward publication.

Thanks to Abby Daly for typing letters to possible publishers and agents.

Thanks to Larry and Starla Flake for nesting me in a secluded writing-room with a view of Lake Conroe.

Thanks to Barbara and LaRoy Hammer for nesting me in a secluded writing-room with a view of the Gulf of Mexico.

Thanks to my editor, Peggy Stautberg, for copyediting and for encouraging me to tell the truth.

Thanks to Faye Walker for her line editing.

Thanks to Tom Hair, owner of Axiom Design of Houston, and designer, Rodney Flores, for creative input.

Thanks to Rita Mills, Project Director and Co-publisher, for being the easiest person in the world with whom to work.

Thanks to John Pack's hawk-eyes for reviewing the final manuscript.

And most of all, thanks to my wife, Patsy, for her patience, flexibility, encouragement, and the kind of feedback that only a loving partner can give.

Preface

I had been a priest for four years when I experienced a crisis of faith, and life's lights went out. Because I believed that ordination had indelibly marked me as a priest for the rest of my years, I thought there was no other life to choose. Although the Church said I could be dispensed from my priestly duties, internally I was shackled. I had no idea how I might make a living as a lay person. Also, I was not sure I could follow my inner promptings without hurting others or suffering their rejection.

I was raised in a thoroughbred Catholic family. Every day before dawn, my mother rose to say the rosary over her tattered prayer books and black coffee at the kitchen table. She also went to daily Mass. While she prayed, my dad was at the produce market preparing to open our grocery store. But his presence at Sunday Mass, with the rest of the family was as assumed as my attendance at school. From an early age, I was taught that the highest calling a young man could answer was to the priesthood, and I took this message to heart. After high school, I resolutely entered a Catholic seminary. Following eight years of training, I was ordained a priest with the understanding that my calling was sealed. And I had been trained not to tamper with the seal through questions or doubts. Because I was ordained when questions and doubts were more commonly recognized as companions, when doubts arose, though I was very hesitant, I did not repress them. That was the beginning of inner rumblings that turned into a quake.

When I recognized that there were tenants of the official church I could no longer express from my heart, I felt hypocritical. I was frozen between the dread of this hypocrisy and my inability to move forward. I read with great relief the words of Anglican Bishop John Robinson in his book *Honest to God:* "All I can do is be honest." The relief was not to last. The honesty that felt like fresh air ushered in other new and unwanted feelings: uncertainty, confusion, and meaninglessness. I went into a frightening free-fall that solidified into a lonely depression. With my substructure severely shaken, I faced the loss of everything that had given my life meaning, and I had nothing with which to replace it.

This led me into therapy, not only to decide whether or not to be a priest but also to find out who I was. It would be two and a half years before I felt I had a footing so that I could decide for something rather than against something. I longed to reach the other side of that desert of uncertainty. Bereft of my personal anchors, I had stopped praying. I wanted the process to cut a clear, straight line, but it was not to be. In those early months, I learned compassion rather than judgment for those who end their own life. I never contemplated suicide, but from that point on I was not quite so mystified by those who do.

I asked for a temporary leave of normal duties while I attended counseling classes at the Institute of Religion in the Texas Medical Center. I would live at a nearby parish rectory, where I said Mass on weekends. The companionship and study at the Institute, and the mutual support of others who grappled with the same issues as I, helped me feel less isolated. It became an exciting time, but I never moved in that wished-for straight line. I often thought of the people I served who would feel let down and some who might judge my motives. If I left the priesthood, how would my family feel about me, and how would they face their friends? I remembered the eight years of spiritual and intellectual preparation for the priesthood, and the question that was put to me by spiritual directors at the end of every year, "Do you freely choose the state to which you aspire?"

When at last I felt I had reached the "other side" of that desert, I found myself, paradoxically, on the very path I always had been on—a path where certainty does not exist without an admixture of uncertainty. And that's where you will find me today. After that two and a half years, I did leave the priesthood, but not the Church, with no bitterness and no regrets. I eventually became a psychotherapist, working with people as I sought to do in the first place.

I share this event from my now distant past because every chapter to follow in this book has its roots in that event and other experiences over the last four decades. An anonymous street poet said that while we like to think of "getting over things," we never do. We live through events that impact us for the rest of our days. I have come to believe that each successive occurrence, if faced, can add colorful strokes to the picture of our lives. This book, then, is an outcropping of my ongoing search, my experience with clients, and the influence of many friends who have searched with me. Since much of the book is of a "how to" nature, a colossal block to writing was the realization of how presumptuous it is for me to tell you how to live your life. The block disappeared when I acknowledged that I am really doing what writers often do—writing to learn something. I have gathered my own philosophy of life together in a form that makes sense to me. The result is a compilation of reflections, guidelines, and reminders to myself of what nurtures and sustains me.

I once counseled a cancer patient in the hospital whose daughter was an artist. Her daughter had some large prints of beautiful watercolors and offered me one of my choosing. A rather surrealistic one of a gazebo surrounded by trees and plants caught my eye. When I asked about the print, she told me that gazebos like that are typically found in town squares south of the border, and that the town square itself is called a zocalo. When she told me that the name of the watercolor was *Finding Your Own Zocalo*, I knew that I wanted it for my office, where people come to find themselves and their place in the world. I hope this book helps all of us come closer to finding our own zocalo.

Introduction

At the end of his counseling session, Robert puts on his jacket, starts for the door, stops, and asks, "What's my homework?" He believes that what he does while away for a week is as important, or more important, than what we do during his counseling hour. Because experience tells me he is on target, I encourage him to make his counseling practical by putting into practice what we talk about. When he does that, he is writing his personal owner's manual for life. I think a lot about how to coach a person to do that, and this book is an outgrowth of some of that thinking. It is about how to create your life when your coach is not around.

I share Robert's wish that on the day of my birth I had come with an owner's manual like the one in the glove box of my car. The manual would tell me what to routinely do for proper care and maintenance so that I would not malfunction, and it would have a section on troubleshooting in case I do. We all recognize the need to follow such a routine to keep our cars and household gadgets in shape. Yet we often assume we need no such manual or routine for our emotional lives, and we pay a great price in purposelessness, depression, and anxiety.

In one sense we are given the equivalent of maintenance instructions from our parents, our religious traditions, and our teachers. But an old principle says that whatever is received is received according to the nature of the receiver. While the sun melts wax, it hardens mud. No matter whose word guides us, it is filtered and acted upon by what we do with it. In that sense, whether aware of it or not, we are constantly creating and re-creating our own owner's manual.

This book is my suggestion, in so far as I know, about how to routinely take the pulse of our lives, to see what we need, to recharge, and redirect. It is a sampling from my owner's manual offered to assist you in making your own. Most of the ideas in this book have been around for centuries, stated and restated by teachers from different disciplines. Some of them may seem strange bedfellows, but I have blended their points of agreement into a workable plan for myself.

Although I'm not particularly adept at fixing cars, I'm drawn to the analogy of car maintenance because so much of life is ordinary, even mechanical. Of course, I also believe that we are vastly greater than our mechanics and that step-by-step prescriptions to our problems are not always available. If we limit ourselves to our mechanics, we miss another part of ourselves, the part that is not under our direct control but has a force, a path, and an intention of its own. This part, recognized by artists and inventors, moves us toward creative expression and can only be reached through intuition. Our "up-keep," then, might better be called artistic, and we, artists. Psychologist Dr. Ira Progoff agrees: "In a profound sense, each human life has the potentiality of becoming an artwork. To that degree, each of us can become an artist-in-life with our finest creation being our own Self."

Sadly we too often identify with the pitiful cartoon character, drooped in a stupor, who says, "My aim is to secure a speaking part in my own life." I would like to tell this character that he is not trapped, not determined by his environment, the economy, the judgments of his employer, or members of his family. These pages are written to help him know that life does not just happen, that he can take the raw materials of his life, experiment with them, shape them, and draw strength and joy from knowing that he does, indeed, have a speaking part in his own life. This book also intends to show him that when he fails, is confused, or despairs, he has access to that other part of himself from which clarity and purpose flow.

So this book is designed to help us become more comfortable on the surface of our lives—jobs, relationships, projects—while also opening a path to our inner self from which these activities flow. It seeks to strike a balance between these two worlds so that on the one hand it is about self-expression, accomplishment, and choice, and on the other about receptivity, discovery, and purpose. The book is divided into two parts: Inhaling and Exhaling. The two parts might be described as listening and taking action. Allowing a continual rhythm of these two stabilizers avoids the pitfalls of too much introspection, which can breed isolation, and too much mindless activity, which can lead to frustrating cul-de-sacs.

Every chapter of the book talks of either my own or someone else's experience in creating our lives and ends with a suggested practice. I strongly encourage you to do the practice or invent one of your own. While most of the exercises are simple, they do require the kind of repetition you would expect in strengthening a muscle.

After hearing about what I was writing, someone said, "Oh, you're showing people how to be their own therapist." I would no more suggest that you be your own therapist than I would suggest that you be your own surgeon. However, if you are in therapy, the book may enhance your counseling hours. If you're not in therapy, the book may serve as a guide to encourage you to take steps into new territory.

Before writing each chapter, I always returned to this question, "What is this book's core purpose?" Over and over, my answer was that this book helps us be who we truly are. Carolyn Meyer, a sculptor in her nineties, created exquisite works of bronze and stone, some she chiseled while leaning from a wheelchair. When asked if she ever doubted what she was to do with her life, her jet-black weathered face gazed straight ahead, and she said, "I was born to sculpt." Hopefully these pages will help us grow in that same conviction of what we were born to be.

Inhaling

CHAPTER 1

Pebbles, Corks, and Beyond

At dawn I gaze eight miles across the chasm, past soft hues on crags and cliffs that plunge beyond sight to the bottom. Our small crowd, warming ourselves under blankets, is silent, as if respecting a holy shrine. The view from the South rim of the Grand Canyon is magnificent, expansive, glorious.

As we leave the site to return to our everyday pedestrian lives, a pebble catches my eye, and I pick it up. I keep this pebble in my office and often show it to clients as a symbol of the part of my mind that is small and shortsighted. The rest of the Canyon, vast and deep, symbolizes the part of my mind that holds more possibilities for life than I can imagine.

I tell clients that when I am at my lowest, thinking I can't manage life or that there isn't much hope, I am thinking within the confines of the pebble when the rest of the Grand Canyon is available to me.

Peeking out of the Pebble

Angela is a buyer for a large department store and the mother of three children. She spearheads projects at work and in her community. Until age forty-two, she was a stranger to gloom. Having descended into depression, she felt suddenly helpless and overwhelmed. Her physician prescribed anti-depressants, but they sat unopened in her medicine cabinet because she didn't believe that her problem originated in her neurotransmitters. Angela came to me to help her unearth the real source of her depression, which she thought might have something to do with her decision to admit her aging mother into a nursing home.

As Angela talked with me about her depression, her problems seemed to grow. Her mother's mortality brought up thoughts of her own mortality, an underlying dissatisfaction with her life, and questions about whether her life meant anything at all. The more she pondered, the more she felt entrapped and enclosed. At the end of one of our sessions, I showed Angela the pebble I'd found at the South Rim. She rolled it in her fingers but didn't seem impressed.

In our next session, Angela surprised me by saying that she had thought a lot about the pebble. She told me that when things felt especially bad during the week she had recalled the image of the Grand Canyon, and it had offered her a ray of hope and freed her to search for new answers. She said she wasn't sure she could move out of the confines of her problems, but at least she was peeking.

Angela's story is a reminder that our minds are twofold, one part much vaster and more resourceful than the other. This is an ancient idea built upon by modern theorists such as Carl Jung, and the image that came to me at the Grand Canyon is a spin-off of an image he proposed.

Jung's Tackle Box

Carl Jung was one of the founders of modern psychiatry, who, it is said, saw meaning in the greatest as well as in the most trivial events. He might have been fishing lazily on Lake Zurich when he caught a metaphor. He said that what we know about ourselves, our conscious minds, is like a cork floating atop the ocean of what we don't know about ourselves, our unconscious. With many others, he theorized that beneath our conscious point of view, there is another reality, an ocean of unrealized potential that strongly influences us for better or worse. When we are aware of that greater part of ourselves, it can be a source of guidance, strength, and inspiration. We need look no further than our daily experience, though, to see how that unconscious part of ourselves can either comfort or confuse us.

Use Your "Hamburger Mind"

Throwing up his hands in despair, a philosophy teacher once accused our college class of having "hamburger minds," meaning we thought too concretely to understand abstract concepts. While he counseled us to put our hamburger minds aside, I encourage you to do the opposite: base your understanding of the concepts in this book on practical experience.

When I first read and heard of our unconscious and how it worked, I found the ideas fuzzy and unrelated to life. My hamburger mind was unsatisfied. After I checked the theory with my experience, though, I had something to sink my teeth into. I invite you to do the same.

We all have experiences that tell us there is more going on than we consciously know. We start the day in a good mood and later wonder what's gotten into us, as if we've been invaded by an outside force. On other days, we feel possessed by a benign spirit and accomplish what we thought we never could. These experiences show us that in addition to what we can see and know objectively, something else is going on below the surface.

Hidden Roots

Jung explains that we are like plants partially visible above ground and partially hidden under ground. Below the surface we have a hidden wellspring of creativity, meaning, and purpose that drives us to become what we are meant to be. It's as if we have within ourselves an inner teacher who gives us ideas, images, and thoughts from which we can learn new and better ways of doing things.

Psychologist Ira Progoff says that part of ourselves is self-regulating and guides us from one point in our lives to another even when we don't understand what it is up to. He observes that "even those beliefs and actions that might be regarded as errors eventually become teachers to us." That inner guide might also be called our "higher self," even our god-self, because attention to it turns normal intelligence into wisdom, leading to answers and solutions we never thought available. Those adept at listening to their own personal teacher are said to have "soul" and their lives are rich with meaning because they tap into what is important to them.

Naming Our Parts and Getting to Know Them

It helps to give the two aspects of ourselves names, and you can take your pick from an array used throughout history. Modern psychology uses "ego" and "unconscious." From this point on, we are going to refer to our conscious point of view as our "ego," and our unconscious point of view as our "source." I like the name "source" because it is dynamic and alive and suggests something not only unknown but also creative.

Our source and ego are comparable to the right and left sides of our brains. Split-brain research tells us that the left side of our brains processes information one piece at a time and has to string those pieces together to see the whole picture, while the right side sees the entire picture at once. Psychologist Adelaide Bry, in her book *Visualization: Directing The Movies of Your Mind,* says that the left side's vision is like that of a person standing near a freight train who sees the train one boxcar at a time. The vision of our right brain is like that of person in a hot air balloon who sees the entire train at once. Our ego sees one boxcar at a time, and our source sees the entire train. Ideally these two sides of ourselves form a partnership, moving us toward the life we are meant to lead.

Our Amphibian Nature

We get a glimpse of this partnership when we work on a problem, put it aside, and suddenly it is resolved when least expected. The ego gathers facts, draws up a working plan, and arranges the facts into what it sees as the solution. But the ego can only go so far, and then it must temporarily bow out and allow the answer to be processed below. That's why often the solution comes to us after a nap, a shower, or a walk. This cooperative effort is always going on, helping us to create the lives we are meant to live. For everything we do on the surface, whether stirring a pot or directing a scalpel, there are inner connections that influence the outcome of what we are doing. That's why it has been said that we have an "amphibian" nature, at home both on the surface and in the depths of our lives. Much of this book deals with how to sustain the partnership between the two.

Our source is working now below the level of our consciousness as I write these lines and as you read them. With my ego I consciously ponder what to say next and how to say it. You read with the conscious intention to add something to your life, or perhaps work through a difficult time. While we consciously go about plotting and planning, our source knows the direction we need to go, what steps to take, and even the problems we will encounter on our way. When we live as if we were only an ego, it's as if we overlook a wise and resourceful person who stands near, willing to hand us answers to questions that otherwise keep us going in circles. When we allow answers to come from within, we are often surprised at their clarity, scope, and relevance, as if they come from something much greater than ourselves.

Even Bigger than the Ocean

Some physicists say these answers do come from a larger source because the unconscious part of ourselves is not limited to the confines of our skin, but is part of an interrelated universe, pulsing with information and energy. While we often speak of connecting to our source within, it may be more accurate to say we are immersed in our source, which is within and all around us, and includes other people and all of nature. Moving out of the pebble, then, means opening to the ideas of others, those in books, as well as those churned out in our own brains.

Belinda's Cosmos

When I was in elementary school, the words "Go see Sister William" would strike terror in me. Sister William was the principal of our school, and her stern gaze was a stun gun that kept us right. As the years passed, though, she softened, exchanged her masculine name for Belinda, and opened up her heart and mind to the world at large. She especially showed a new interest in scientific inquiry and philosophy. Several years ago, we reconnected and remained friends until she died at the age of ninety-five.

One detail of our relationship that sticks out in my memory is Belinda's fascination with computers and the Internet. I remember how excitedly she described the phenomenon of someone in the United States instantly accessing information and pictures from Australia. She said she thought we were seeing what theologians and philosophers have said all along, that while we think we are separate, our lives extend beyond our vision because the universe is one piece.

She also was mesmerized by the so-called new physics that spoke about the oneness of reality. We talked at length about how some "new" ideas are really not all that new. The great spiritual message always has been that we take our cues from a source greater than ourselves and that we are part of that greater source.

Confession to a Librarian

Dr. Ruth Fry, co-founder of the Jung Educational Center in Houston, liked to put the right book into the hands of the right person at the right time. When I was at my lowest, she handed me a book by Ira Progoff called *The Death and Rebirth of Psychology.* The author opens: "Although it began as part of the protest against religion, the net result of modern psychology has been to reaffirm man's experience of himself as a spiritual being." When I read that, I never even paused. Faced with whether or not to be a priest, I was more interested in getting on with the rest of the book and getting some "real" answers.

I kept the book for years before returning it. Later, when I got my own copy and reread Progoff's opening sentence, I thought, "Wow!" The statement suddenly made sense to me. I had lived a few years with Jung's idea about the cork and the ocean and had begun the slow process of pulling old spiritual ideas out of the garbage can. As I retrieved them, I saw them in a new way. I realized that the essence of spirituality is that I am part of something infinitely greater than what I see. Faith is a creative springboard out of my accustomed boundaries where I am always smarter than I think, more resourceful than I dream, and my available good far outweighs my expectations.

So psychology helped lead me back to a solid spirituality, which I now see is good psychology, and for me their message is the same. That message is an invitation to something greater, more meaningful, and more fulfilling. Rather than a call to some static plateau or some state of perfection, it is a summons to ride the inevitable roller coaster of life.

A Walk Through the Canyon

When in touch with our source, the path we follow has been compared to walking through a maze because of the unknown and unpredictable elements we encounter, rather like the trail through the Grand Canyon itself. Sometimes we move easily from one step to another. But often we take detours and find ourselves in regions we had not counted on and through which we prefer not to travel. We weave in and out of joy and depression, pride and embarrassment, clarity and confusion. When our source and ego are open to each other's influence, we can minimize the detours and the frustration of those we can't avoid.

With the two aspects of ourselves in sync, we are not likely to go far down a path before recognizing it is not our own. Or we may see that while suitable for a time, it's no longer the path we want. When we expect twists and turns, we don't wear ourselves out fighting every unsought change. We trust that problems and events fit into a grander scheme and may take longer to work through than we would like and that the most fulfilling outcome may be different than we thought.

Back to Our Experience

Because the ideas in this chapter are a way to make sense of what we daily experience, I strongly suggest that you allow them to be validated in light of what happens in your own life. Our experience tells us that things are certainly not always what they seem, that life's picture is bigger than our perception. We know that often when we stop pushing and striving, we see answers and bits of meaning coming from unexpected directions. We may never understand how this happens. What is important is that we grow in the realization that there is so much more to our world than our conscious point of view, and there is always more room for trust, dreams, and openness.

In other words, we continue to learn that what we call our "self" is only part of our Self, that there is much more beyond the pebble. When we do that, our egos recognize something beyond themselves—our indefinable center and source.

Practice this—

1. For the next few days, imagine you are living inside a pebble at the bottom of the Grand Canyon, and if you step out of the pebble you will begin to discover all you need so that you can be the person you are meant to be. That greater canyon holds possibilities beyond your vision—long-term solutions, and clues to the meaning of your life. When you step out, you feel the difference in your body and mind because you are more at peace, loose, and light. While in the pebble,

where your vision is short-sighted, you are more restless, stiff, and tight.

2. Reflect on that image as you begin your day, giving it a few minutes to sink in. You can do this in the shower or while driving to work. Focus on the enormity of the canyon of possibilities and the smallness of what you can see in the pebble. Don't try to figure out how this might be. Simply hold the image as a reflection of how your mind works. Before letting the image go, say to yourself, "There is so much more than I can see," or "There are so many more possibilities than I can see." During the day, recall the image and ask yourself whether you are focusing within the pebble or opening to the rest of the canyon. As you do that, repeat the above phrases or something similar.

CHAPTER 2

Stepping Outside the Pebble

On the phone, Russell clears his throat and nervously moves down his list of questions designed to check me out: How old are you? Are you married? Do you believe in God? Do you have children? What school of behavior do you follow?

I tell Russell that I favor any viewpoint that recognizes that we are full of possibilities, that if we work, play, and follow our passions, we will more easily tap those possibilities and become the people we are meant to be. In other words, I like schools of thought that remind us of how creative we are.

I don't mean that our mental health depends upon proficiency in the arts or sciences. I do mean to say that the more we realize that we have the option to step out of the "pebble" to find our gifts, talents, and sense of purpose, the more content we will be. If we are in touch with our innate creativity, we may not choose to paint, but life will be more colorful. We may not play music, but we'll be more lyrical. We may not be scientifically innovative, but our lives will never lack possibilities.

Starting with What's Right with You

Often our first call to a therapist is made with fear—fear of being analyzed, dissected, picked apart. Already Russell had been beating himself up, asking, "What's wrong with me?" And he was stuck in an "if only" groove. "If only I had more money. If only I had a better job. If only I had a different house," and the list goes on. He may as well have said, "If only I were someone else." Russell was not cracked, in need of being pieced back together. Rather, he had forgotten who he was and that he was so much more than he could see. So it was a relief for him to hear that we would be focusing on what's right with him.

A creative approach asserts that behind every problem, such as anxiety, depression, or meaninglessness, lies a part of ourselves that we have blocked. If a drain is clogged, our only reason for giving the blockage attention is to remove it so that the flow of clear water can resume. That's why we will rarely unearth our personal treasures in a weekly exploration of what happened, what went wrong, and how bad we feel. That kind of focus keeps us cramped inside the pebble. We need to be coached out of the pebble to a place where we can say, "Because I have so many resources, I can choose a new direction." When we recognize how well put together we already are, negative symptoms can be flags that call us to a more creative life.

What Motivates You Out of Bed?

Psychologist Dr. Lawrence Le Shan tells cancer patients that what they most need is to concentrate on what motivates them out of bed in the morning. In doing so, they will be able to live from deep inside, past the learned rules of conformity that keep them thinking the same old thoughts and coming to the same old conclusions. That sense of purpose, of moving somewhere that means something to us, is the fire of a creative person's life.

When we are alive to our own creativity, we are "entheos," "in God," always generative. Rather than dream of securing a speaking part in our lives, we build, write, paint, and contribute. Life is not problem-free, but neither is it problem-oriented. When we are in that creative mode, we are far better at thinking about what we want than what we don't want.

There is an easy way to check out whether we are following Le Shan's advice. We can ask ourselves what the rest of this day or tomorrow holds for us. What answers come up? Do we see only problems on the horizon? Are we preoccupied with how to make it through the day or night? With a little shift in our thinking, we can operate with a sense of direction that permeates all we do. With that vision we may not get ecstatic over cleaning the kitty litter box, but our hours as a whole will be more satisfying, and we'll open to more joy. And that vision, coming from the seat of our passion, will spawn another trait of creative living, openness to possibilities.

A Mind Full of Possibilities

When a sense of profound helplessness led me to a therapist, I came to see why depression is often referred to as "black." Depression ushered me into a hopelessly hemmed-in place of no visible possibilities. There was no satisfaction in what I had, no future, and no road toward one. Joy was inaccessible, and I sank into a dark place that was hard to escape. When wondering what I would do with myself if I were not a priest, I recall thinking that maybe I could sell shoes. That's how far out of the pebble I could see. Then my ego intervened and said, "Nope, you can't even do that. You don't know enough about math to calculate a discount if a friend buys your shoes." Deeper into the pebble I went.

I'm not so sure how to tell you how I came out of that darkness, but I'm certain that it had a lot to do with opening myself to possibilities even before I could see what they might be. Then I could affirm the most my fearful ego would allow: "Maybe there's a way." With that crack in the exit door, I shifted more in the direction of "I can," rather than "I can't."

Another Way to Move a File Cabinet

I once asked the participants in a seminar to tell about ways they had experienced creativity in their lives. A man told about how one day when he came home from work, he noticed that his wife had moved a huge steel file cabinet from its downstairs location to the study upstairs. Since two men would have had a difficult time moving it, he wondered how his petite wife accomplished the job. She explained that after removing the drawers, she was able to slide the cabinet on the carpet to the bottom of the stairs. She then tied a long garden hose around it, took the slack upstairs and threw it out a window. Outside, she tied the loose end to the bumper of her car, slowly drove the car forward, stopping three or four times to get out and check her progress up the stairs, until she had successfully moved the hulk to the second floor.

This woman shows us what happens when we are willing to open to possibilities. She broke some cultural rules that could have held her back: "Women don't move big file cabinets. Even my strong husband couldn't do it alone." Because she didn't consult that rulebook, but rather listened for possibilities suggested from within herself, she got the job done. She called on that part of herself that insists, "There must be a way to do this."

That part is more vocal when we are very young. I remember when my boys were small and they would ask me to make something on my workbench for them to play with. If I said that I couldn't, they would say, "Yes, you can!" Sometimes I'd listen to them, delightfully surprised at the finished product. Children are better at seeing possibilities than many adults.

Play

If you want to turn the heat up on your creativity, reclaim what you left on your father's workshop floor. What you'll find there are creations that came from our ability to play. Every work of art, every new discovery, was birthed because of someone's playful urge. Play is confidently flexing and exploring rather than rigidly following assigned ruts. When we play, we can more easily do what psychologist Carl Rogers suggests, toy with elements and ideas. Mistakes don't stop us because, when playful, we expect to set out, run into dead ends, and try again. With every try, we gain more information and hone our skills a bit.

I once spoke with Dr. John Lienhard, engineer and author of the public radio spot *The Engines of Our Ingenuity*. His program on exploring "how inventive minds work" had risen to national fame, and I wanted to pick his brain about creativity. As we sat over coffee in his study, he gave me two articles, both of which were on the constructive use of failure. One of the articles Dr. Lienhard gave me told the story of someone asking Edison how he could stand to fail nine hundred and ninety-nine times before, on the thousandth try, he produced one of his greatest hits, the light bulb. His response was that he hadn't failed at all. He had nine hundred and ninety-nine experiences that led him to success.

My Mother and Thomas Edison

My mother had a bit of Edison in her when in the kitchen. The stresses of family finances and running our grocery store made her fret and worry. But she entered her kitchen a fearless, playful artist. Always in motion and in spite of spills, she enjoyed the process. When giving us a recipe, she would say, "A little olive oil, a bit of oregano, a handful of basil." She never offered exact measurements. She taught us, "If you don't like it, throw it away and try again." I remember her in her eighties teaching me to make Italian sausage. She suddenly turned to me and exclaimed, "Isn't this fun!" Because I had that playful and experimental attitude modeled in the kitchen, I, too, am comfortable there and am rarely at an impasse. When I go there, I don't see work. I see possibilities for good food. I have learned that what I call lack of talent or know-how in other areas is really my hesitancy to play in unfamiliar territory.

Serious Play

Play is not always humorous and lighthearted. We need creative ways to deal with tragedy, work through grief, find alternatives to violence, and face pain. I've known cancer patients who have managed to approach their disease with a sense of play. Virginia had advanced liver cancer and was often attached to IVs and a portable pump. She became known in the hospital for her ingenious ways of rigging these attachments so that she could continue to participate actively in life. Humor was her hallmark. She said, "If you don't hit tragedy head on with fun, you'll smother under it." She told me with a thick Louisiana accent of how she made it alone through the Houston airport. "At first I couldn't find anyone to carry my things. Then I said aloud to an attendant, 'Honey, you know I have cansa,' and fifteen porters converged on all my bags." If we can hold onto our sense of creative play even when the stakes are high, we not only avoid bitterness and despair, but solutions are far more apparent. Unfortunately, our "no pain, no gain" philosophy tells us that the mark of virtue is the level of agony we can tolerate.

When I decided to learn to write, I bought lots of books on writing to see how others did it. Almost without exception, the authors said that they did not enjoy writing, but rather, they enjoyed having written. The process of getting to the enjoyment was full of anxiety, confusion, and doubt. At first, I was glad to know that I, a hesitant fledgling, had something in common with great writers, our misery. But in time this common bond was less consoling, not only because it didn't feel good, but because I found misery to be anticreative. It is encouraging to know that most great writers have to work hard, and I expect to, also. But for me, when work is equated with despondency, the result I hope for is not only delayed but stiff. Now I don't care to write unless I enjoy it. I don't always get what I want and stringing these words together is sometimes just hard work. But my goal is to yoke work and fun together. That not only feels better but the end product has more heart and life.

Creative Sweat

Marie told me that when she started her real estate business, she planned to work every other day so that she could golf and relax on her days off, giving her "inner child" lots of time to play. She was determined not to let work keep her from life's pleasures as her father had done. Her business floundered for a year and almost collapsed until she began to put more time into it. At first, she was resentful that she had to work so hard, but, eventually, she learned to hit a balance between play and work. Listening to that child within ourselves can save us from rigid adherence to useless structure and rules. But if we insist on a steady diet of cheer, we stay in our well worn, boring grooves.

Athletes and artists will tell you that the reason their work looks easy is because great effort went into it. After a performance, an adoring fan told a virtuoso violinist that he would give his life to play like that. The musician responded, "I did." When we are willing to do what it takes, we will usually sweat. That certainly is true for our greatest work of art, ourselves. There is the mental anguish of going against the crowd, of moving beyond one's own comfort zone. There is the grief of giving something up to get something new. There is the physical toll of tight muscles, nerves, and fatigue, all part of a day's work. The trick is to welcome both that playful child and the hard-working adult but not let either take over. It seems that what we sometimes call "goofing off" is essential to creativity. If you're a couch potato, you may have already mastered an important skill.

Creative Couch Potatoes

A certain amount of down time is required not only because of fatigue, but because down time seems to be essential to creativity. Much of the music we enjoy, the technology that enhances our lives, are, by the creator's account, the fruit not only of hard work, but of idleness. There are countless examples of creative works falling into place when the person wasn't working, but rather doing something unrelated to his masterpiece. Michael Samuels, in his book *Seeing with the Mind's Eye,* says that the common denominator of inspirational states is one of relaxed attention: walking at leisure, dreaming. Researchers have concluded that time away from work, cultivating receptive as well as active states of mind, is essential to the creative process. Some regard it as the heart of creativity.

That puts most of us at risk. When Mozart was riding in his horse and carriage, he didn't have a cell phone on, and while Poincare walked the bluff at the seaside, he wasn't wearing a pager. Often what we consider "essential" blots out the stillness and silence that lead to creativity.

Up and Down Time

The philosopher Plotinus said that we are amphibians, at home in two different worlds: the underworld of the spirit and the outer world of action. A creative person is awake to the signals from his source and uses his ego and rational brain to live what he hears. Ira Progoff says such a person lives a rhythm of action and receptivity on the journey but at times idles at a well for replenishment. That person's lifestyle reflects a combination of monk and entrepreneur as he is given to action, planning, and thought as well as to meditation, reverie, and flights of imagination.

So you will find the creative person actively grinding away putting things together, taking them apart, lost in what he is doing. You may find the same person immersed in meditation, music, walking, giving no thought to his projects. For most of us, this rhythm gets easier the more we rehearse the side with which we are least familiar.

James, for instance, was good at working hard but not so practiced at resting. He felt more creative when he learned to leave what he was doing for a while. At first, this was difficult because he associated a pause from work with laziness. The story about the woodsman who found his work increasingly difficult but claimed he was too busy to sharpen his ax helped him. As we will see, the rest periods are necessary not only to rejuvenate us but also to allow unseen forces to do their work.

Beth was much better at resting and letting things take their own course. She found it easy to dream, to leave her creative engine on idle but found actually doing the work in her interior design shop less appealing. This was no problem as long as she had a partner for whom taking action was more natural. When she and her partner parted ways, she thought she would have to find another career. But with the willingness to practice doing what she thought she was not so good at her dreams more often became reality. Both Beth and James found that they did not have to give up the side they were good at. The balance meant more of a partnership for both within themselves.

Taking Your Creative Pulse

These five traits of a creative person can serve as a checklist to help us stay on an inventive track. Whenever I'm hesitant, at a standstill, or find that I'm going in circles with a project or issue, I can usually find the difficulty by seeing which of the five I'm neglecting. You can do this by using the following practice.

Practice this—The following questions can help you know whether you are following a creative path.

1. Am I open to possibilities?
2. Am I having fun?
3. Am I working?
4. Am I resting?
5. Am I balancing work and rest?

CHAPTER 3

Both / And

A client once brought me a news article that she said finally explained her difficulty. The article reported on a symposium of the American Psychological Association entitled "The Overlooked Virtues of Negativity." That symposium addressed the backfiring effect of trying to be positive when so much of life is hard. The article said that the pressure imposed by some writers and speakers who encourage us to be happy, "or worse, act happy, when we are not, is very stressful." I found the article delightful and its point well taken. But I was weary of my client's and the reporter's conclusion: that all this proves it's better to be negative than positive. Whatever happened to Aristotle's "Virtue lies in the middle way?" Why not make room for being both positive and negative since life is not only hard but also joyful? The failure to find balance in our thinking, not only in this area but in all areas, is responsible for more problems than we know.

Ancient Wisdom, Common Feeling

That balance is so important that in the fifteenth century the philosopher Giordono Bruno called it the "indispensable key to the universe." This ancient idea tells us that the universe is made of opposites:

light and dark, masculine and feminine, rational and irrational. These polarities are easy to see within ourselves. We are often cock-sure while at the same time doubtful. Part of us wants to move on, and part wants to stay put. At once we love and hate, are resolute and lazy.

While we often try to adhere to one side or the other, experts tell us that creative people are at home with these seemingly contradictory things, that their inventiveness actually stems from the acceptance of such opposites. Because inventive people are comfortable with different and even "crazy" ideas, they can allow what seems foreign to couple with what is familiar to make something new. Creativity, then, is like the chemical reaction that occurs when two different elements come together to form a new substance. I am referring to this idea now not only because it is an essential tool of creativity but because without it many of the ideas in this book may seem elusive and contradictory.

Confusion or Enlightenment?

Already we have talked about the foundation of opposites within ourselves, that we are both conscious and unconscious. This could be more confusing than helpful because it calls us to follow our own preferences as well as our unseen guiding spirit, to make choices and to listen. If we can accept that our very fabric contains these opposites, we can accept all the other opposites that give birth to new ideas, workable lifestyles, relationships, works of art, and careers.

While I am now more comfortable with this balance between my own conscious and unconscious self, in the past it was more of a struggle. Should I be a man of reflection or a man of action, I wondered? When I became interested in psychology, I ran into a similar challenge because I was reminded of the freedom I had not only to make conscious choices but also of how short-sighted those choices can be without guidance from my source. Was I to forge ahead with my own plans or wait for my source to direct me?

Looking for the Partnership Within

Searching bookstores for answers, I found two camps: one that valued the inner world, leading me down what some authors call a spiritual path, and another camp that valued the external world, leading me down what many call a material path. One camp encouraged meditation and the proverbial "going with the flow." The other camp preached the value of organization and clearly defined goals. Depending on which book I read, I might have concluded that either the inner-directed or the outer-directed one was the "right" one.

I noticed myself leaning to one side and then another. In doing so, I found that I made enemies because I left "the others" on the other side. When I became more aggressive, I thought that my reflective friends should get real, not meditate so much, and do something. When I decided that I was the one who should meditate more, I would think that my action-oriented friends were too identified with their egos, too shallow, and should dream more.

While I now believe that this struggle is one of life's constant challenges, I find great peace when I can accept that my ego and source are complementary and form a partnership. When I rely only on my ego, without stopping to listen or reflect, attempts to create life differently go in endless circles. Confined to the surface of my life, I repeatedly cover the same ground. If I neglect the use of my ego and do not exercise choices, I remain aimless. That's why this book respects both sides of our amphibian nature and suggests ways to live a rhythm of inward and outward activity.

Better to Inhale or Exhale?

Ira Progoff says that going inward is like going down a well, where we find renewal and strength. When we go to those depths, we don't stay there, but with the insights acquired we move on and in time stop to go down the well again. We accept this rhythm as we do the cycles of the seasons, the diastole and systole beats of our hearts, inhaling and exhaling. Indeed, some problems have a way of evaporating when we realize that what we are pondering is like asking "Is it better to inhale or exhale?" When a person lives this rhythm, he works with the natural freedom of an artist whose acceptance of both his ego and source is a journey of choice and discovery.

The Mind's Rhythm on Canvas

If an artist paints a broad red line at the top of a canvas because that's what he feels like doing, he is painting by preference. If he adds other colors and shapes in hopes of producing an image that corresponds to the image in his mind, the process of chosen art continues. However, he soon discovers things in the picture he had not planned, perhaps the result of mistakes, or things that, once they are on the canvas, have a different shape, texture, or mood than his image and are more beautiful than planned. So the picture begins to head in its own direction, and the artist happily and willingly follows with subsequent strokes of the brush. Soon he again begins to deliberately choose colors and shapes that he consciously feels are right for the picture. When the picture is finished, he will have shifted his stance several times, allowing for an interplay of two influences in his mind—his ego and source. So the acceptance of opposites can turn into a creative force. The above analogy applies equally to following a career, raising a family, changing a tire or a diaper. Here is a workaday example of how a potential war in the soul can become the same kind of creative force.

The Same Rhythm on the Job

A client I'll call William had successfully climbed the corporate ladder and sought a Masters in Business Administration so he could climb faster and higher. He couldn't find time to brush up on material for the entrance exam because he didn't want to give up time at work. He decided to take the exam going on what he knew, and, to the surprise of his friends, he failed.

Normally, William kept a watch on thoughts and hunches that threatened his chosen course, not allowing them to pass the gate of his consciousness. This time, though, I suggested he had nothing to lose by entertaining the foreign thoughts because he didn't have to act on them. William began to imagine what it would be like to change course and pursue a different career.

As he allowed various images to play in his mind, he had recollections of himself as a child standing before beautiful buildings, dreaming of being an architect before he knew what the word meant. The more he dreamed, the more fascinated he became, buying books on architecture and talking to people in that field. Six months later, he found himself in the office of the dean of admissions at the University of Houston School of Architecture. He knew the switch would be difficult, but he had the motivation that comes from being true to one's own aspirations. This experience helped teach William how acceptance of his internal contradictions could move him forward.

The Ultimate Balance

My greatest teachers of this important principle have been people who have had to live the ultimate balance of life and death, cancer patients. When I first began to counsel with these patients, I often found myself in a dilemma. On the one hand, patients were being told that a positive attitude and a strong will to live could extend their lives. On the other hand, they were encouraged to make peace with death, to approach it openly and consciously. I was puzzled about when to stop counseling patients to live and begin helping them to die.

The clearest answer came from those patients who instinctively knew the answer. While many patients fell to one side or the other, either giving up hope or denying the diagnosis, others could keep their balance. I am talking about people like Mark, who was told by the best specialists in California to get his affairs in order because he had only a few months to live. He planned his funeral, cried with his family, told them goodbye. Then he began a search for a doctor who would offer him hope and treatment. He found such a doctor in now retired Dr. John S. Stehlin, Jr., at St. Joseph's Hospital in Houston, where I counseled patients. After being treated by Dr. Stehlin, Mark lived for ten years to the amazement of the doctors who originally diagnosed him.

The Challenge of the Twin Towers

This ultimate tension has thrust itself into the lives of Americans with the attack on New York's Twin Towers. Many of my clients have mentioned the attack, some acknowledging that it stopped their lives in their tracks. John came for counseling stunned by those events and noticed that heightened security at airports and the promise of a strong military defense did not relieve him. He came to see that what snagged him was the realization of how easily it all happened. And if this could happen, what else? If in New York, why not Houston? I talked to him about Mark, the cancer patient who seemed to know how to go on with life though life was side by side with death. I told him that I had picked Mark's brain and asked him how he could choose to go ahead with plans for a new house after having been given such a grim diagnosis. Mark's answer was that before his diagnosis he came to know that life does not stretch on forever and that he had never been promised the next day. He said that as long as he lived the illusion that life held no threat of interruption, there was a kink in everything he did, something that sapped his energy. While one part of him skipped along, the other part was unconsciously busy holding off "the bad guys," his mistakes and blunders, the intrusions of others, even death itself. To the extent that he could give up the struggle against his dual nature and accept it, he had more energy.

The Stuff of Life

Because we are never free of internal conflict and because those conflicts can be transforming, psychologist John Sanford says they are the "stuff of life." Yet we wear ourselves out trying to reach some kind of peaceful state where there is no internal opposition. But real peace is the peace between the inevitable opposing forces within ourselves, especially between the opposing forces of our ego and source. And in our culture, that kind of peace is rare. While we often talk of having an open mind, what we are open to is what we are most conscious of, those things that support our already formed plans, ideas, and traditions. When we allow the co-existence of opposites within ourselves, we may still feel tension, but it is the expected tension we feel when getting somewhere. Jung says that if we hold the tension of our opposites, transformation occurs. Holding that tension sets in motion the natural ability of our minds to arrive at a new attitude. I find this a refreshing alternative to trying to avoid dilemmas, especially those thorny ones: How much for me and how much for others? Do I work or play? Should I be a man of the spirit or of the world?

When You Can Reach for the Stars

Often when sorting out a problem or working through a transition, something comes into our lives that acts as a confirmation that we are on the right track. It might be the example of a friend, the words of a song, a movie, or a book. The stage play *Man of La Mancha* together with reflections on the play by Episcopal priest R. Calvert Rutherford, Jr. was such an event for me. The pivot of the play is Don Quixote's relationship with the angry and bitter local whore Aldonza. Quixote is considered mad because of his excessive imagination, especially when he imagines himself as a knight in shining armor and regards Aldonza as his pure and beautiful Dulcinea. She insists that she is not pure and beautiful, as others insist that there are no longer any knights in shining armor. While at first she is thrown into despair over his vision, in the end she is transformed and accepts herself as a person of worth and dignity.

Rutherford says that Quixote is able to stretch beyond what our eyes can see because he uses both/and thinking rather than either/or thinking. Either/or thinking strives for certainty and will latch onto anything that keeps intact what we already know. It is exclusive, constricting, and threatened by too much imagination. Both/and thinking is comfortable with uncertainty, open to viewpoints outside the "pebble" of awareness, and imagination is its fuel.

Technically called a reductionist, the either/or thinker reduces everything to its basest explanation, and his language is filled with the word "only." Rutherford says, "A sunset is only clouds and the sensible man is interested only in whether or not they bring rain. A painting is only daubs of color, unless the resale value is high. People are only children, only women, only farmers, only foolish visionaries. Unheroic and pedestrian, the reductionist neither dreams dreams nor tolerates those who do." So our ability to dream the impossible rests on both/and thinking.

Practice this—

1. Notice any indecision, dilemmas, or conflicts in your life. You may be undecided about what to do. You may have mixed feelings about a person. It may be difficult to make peace within yourself between independence and dependence, assertiveness, and passivity. Make a list if that helps. As you notice each conflict, rather than resist it or berate yourself for it, practice accepting the conflict as the beginning of something new. For the next few days whenever these or other conflicts arise, simply notice and accept them. As you do this, see if there is a difference in how you feel about them or if they are resolved anymore efficiently.

2. Here is another way to do the same thing that I once learned from a therapist with whom I counseled. Sit quietly with your eyes closed and think of a conflict. Imagine one decision to the right of you and the opposite one to your left. You might imagine holding one in your right hand and its opposite in your left. Imagine the two of them peacefully in your possession. Then imagine a bright fire between the two so that the

fire begins to consume and meld the two together and that all you can then see is the fire as it continues to transform the opposites into a new attitude, a new way of seeing, a new way of being. Trust that as you let the image go, the process is happening within you. When you find yourself obsessing about the conflict, recall the image of the fire within yourself and turn your attention to something else.

CHAPTER 4

The Touchstone

The Sioux Indian Lame Deer says, "Only human beings have come to the point where they no longer know why they exist." A fable tells us why this is so. The fable is about a school for animals where each animal is required to learn various skills without regard for what each, by nature, does best. The tale proceeds:

> Mr. Squirrel was the best student in the climbing class. He was also good at running. But flying was very difficult for him because he had to start from the ground up. His repeated attempts at take-offs gave him charley horses, which had a bad effect on his other subjects. His grades in climbing fell to Cs. He barely passed running.
>
> Ms. Duck was an excellent swimmer. In the water, she had more talent and skill than the teacher. Her work in flying class was satisfactory. But she had serious difficulty in running and couldn't seem to catch on to climbing at all. Because of her low grades in running and climbing, she had to stay after school for extra practice. This meant giving up swimming lessons. Her grade in swimming fell to a C. Her

teacher thought that was fine. Average is almost always acceptable.

At the beginning of the semester, Ms. Rabbit was the top student in the running class. No matter how hard she tried, she couldn't keep up with classmates in swimming and flying. She got so far behind with make-up work that she had a nervous breakdown and had to drop out of school.

Mr. Eagle was a discipline problem. His teachers said he had a bad attitude. In swimming class, he refused to go in the water. In climbing class, he was so determined to get to the top of the tree first that he used an unacceptable method for getting there. He flew up. He hated school.

Why Squirrels do Better than We do

A cartoon by Ashleigh Brilliant says, "I was educated once and it took me years to overcome it." When Mr. Squirrel awakens in the morning, he has no conflict about priorities. He never struggles over whether it is best to gather nuts or hang out at the bird feeder, and he certainly never has the urge to do things painfully against a squirrel's nature like swim a few laps in the pool. So what happened to us?

Children live naturally in an open stance and don't stop every idea in its tracks to question it to death. If they want to build a fort, they do so without thinking about obstacles. They move energetically to the finish, proud of the rickety, unbalanced structure of mismatched wood, tin, and cardboard. Then they hear, "Shouldn't you paint it? Don't you know nails cost money?" Suddenly the focus shifts from "I can't wait to build a fort," to "If I do, it will be a piece of junk." While we envy the pure spontaneity of children, we also know they need guidance. But if that guidance leads them to believe that their way is wrong and everyone else's is correct, the child begins to live only by rules that keep others happy. They begin to follow a script or drama lived from rote rather than from the heart.

We begin to play happy when sad and sad when happy, to assume the role of accountant when we were born to paint, or paint when we were born to juggle numbers. We fall prey to a mass hypnotism, and the right thing becomes what movie critics say, what the fashion experts prescribe, what the spin doctors dictate. Noticing how all-embracing this conformity can be. Philosopher Arthur Schopenhauer said, "We forfeit three fourths of our lives to be like someone else." Because the rules we lived by to gain acceptance were put in place early in life, we may have long since forgotten them. But they are there, subtle and engrained, influencing everything we do.

Crazy-Making Facts

In the stage play *Man of La Mancha,* Don Quixote remarks, "Facts are the enemy of truth." We often think we know this or that about ourselves and others. But often we're simply mouthing scripts we made up years ago to gain acceptance. Resting in our minds like slides in a projector, these images cast a shadow on everything we see, so that people, events, and circumstances are shaped by them. Those images are the "facts" of our lives. They determine what we can and can't do, what we feel, what a man or woman is, whether the world is hostile or loving. They are powerful, far sweeping, and may have no resemblance to the truth. Because scripts were originally our guardians and we unconsciously depend upon them for stability, we often choose them over reality, whether good for us or not. Unexamined scripts are the basis of discord in families and even war between nations because they encourage self-righteousness and disallow negotiation.

Knowing the origin of unconscious scripts is not always necessary. But we do need to know that they may be lurking in the background, pumping up our egos, foretelling misfortune, pitting us against others. Those scripts feed rage, depression, and anxiety, and they take us far astray from our true nature.

Will the Real Me Please Stand?

I first realized the extent to which unworkable rules that had hardened into "facts" were directing the course of my life when I began questioning the unquestionable: "Once a priest, always a priest." Before that time, my path was pretty well mapped out with not many clouds in sight, and I never dreamed I would one day be taking my life apart and piecing it back together. I told my therapist that I felt like a disassembled car engine whose parts were strung out on the lawn, and I wasn't sure what to do with them. I also told him of my fear and confusion because I could not say with certainty where I would be the following year. He gently welcomed me to planet earth. Part of my problem was that the old assumptions I had built my life upon had fallen apart, and it hadn't yet occurred to me how to replace them or that I even could.

I also remember talking for hours with my friend John, who had an enormous influence on me by constantly interjecting, "But who said so?" when I talked about the rigid theological and personal rules that bound me. At first, I was irritated. It was months before I could acknowledge that he was asking a pretty good question. The answer to "Who said so," was almost always someone else—other people, the church, never myself. That, of course, made everyone else responsible for my unhappiness. What I finally faced was a deep-seated belief that I didn't have the right to think much for myself. That belief, along with other beliefs, was in the driver's seat as long as it was unconscious and unquestioned. After questioning it, I could then begin sorting out the real me from the adapted me.

But it was not as easy as standing over those disassembled parts saying, "Let's see; I'll take this one and toss that one; that one seems to suit me but that other one doesn't," until Humpty Dumpty was back together. I moved haltingly into the alien territory of personal responsibility. Sometimes I felt the shock of jumping into a cold swimming pool: "Oh God, why did I jump?" Often decisions from my own gut were accompanied by fear and grief. I feared making the wrong decision, being disloyal, or hurting others. I grieved the loss of certainty, the familiarity of the old ways, and the absolute approval of others.

The Task Beneath Every Task

During that sorting period, I told my therapist that I was worried about becoming selfish, shifting from a belief that everyone else was right and I was wrong, to a belief that I was right and everybody else was wrong. He told me that I would find that if I did what was really right for me, it would be right for others. Inside me, his words seemed to unblock a vessel. I knew he was saying something that was on the mark.

When he spoke of what was *really* right for me, I knew he meant something beyond my ego, that greater source of which we are all a part. The genius of Shakespeare, almost a cliché, hit me: "This above all: to thine own self be true, then it must follow as the night the day, thou cans't not be false to any man." Not "you might not" but "you cannot." So I knew that all that sorting was not just a decision for one lifestyle over another. It was a search for my own identity. Over and over, I would see that what Jung said of that search was true, that it is *the* task of life.

And the task is never finished. There would be constant reminders that I had not arrived: recurrent doubt, fear, and depression. I am still learning to see these revisits not as punishment or reminders of how wrong I am but simply as more welcome signs to planet earth. If I merely hold them at bay, I risk emotional infection. If I face them, I discover deeper meaning. This slant on life's messy side is artfully stated in Jungian analyst Dr. James Hollis' book, aptly named *Swamplands of the Soul—New Life in Dismal Places.*

Joseph Campbell and Rosetta's Hairstylist

During the TV series *The Power of Myth,* journalist Bill Moyers asked Joseph Campbell about how we go about finding our true selves. Campbell said, "I always tell my students, go where your body and soul want to go. When you have the feeling, then stay with it, and don't let anyone throw you off."

I know a seventy-five-year-old lady, Rosetta, who heard that a local center for the homeless was looking for volunteers, and she applied. The director of the center knew that Rosetta was interested in painting and asked her to teach an art class. Rosetta said that she'd love to do that but didn't feel she had enough talent to teach art although the director insisted she was just the person the center needed.

Later that week, while Rosetta was being clipped and styled, her hairstylist noticed a worrisome look and asked what was on her mind. She told him the story and of her disappointment at not being able to take advantage of a wonderful opportunity. His response was: "Well, there's no reason you can't do this job because I've seen your work, and you have what it takes. Besides, whatever you genuinely don't know how to do, I will teach you. I'm an art teacher." Today, five years later, she continues to do what she loves, teaching art at that homeless center. While I know many people who have made choices similar to Rosetta's, not all of them did it easily. A common complaint was that they had no motivation.

When Jeffery Felt Like a Slug

Jeffery, the owner of an antique store, said he hadn't felt motivated to do much for several years. He had no hobbies, his store was the focal point of his life, and duty brought him unexcitedly to his children's soccer games and school activities. He said he felt like a slug, especially in the morning as he dragged himself out of bed to begin his day. Once he got started, he managed to keep going but with no spark and little humor. When I asked him about his business, his face wrinkled as if he had smelled a foul odor, and he said he hated it. The only reason he sold antiques was because the store had been in the family for generations, and he felt obligated to keep it going. When I asked if he could sell the business and do something more to his liking, he protested that was impossible.

Slowly, though, Jeffery came to see that it was quite possible for him to sell his store and do something else. He had just never allowed himself to seriously consider doing so. His script told him, "If it feels bad, do it," and he could see his father living those words. Changing that belief restored his motivation for living, and he felt much less like a slug. He began to have a feeling that for him was strange: excitement, not only about his new work but about other things in his life, too.

Quarterbacks and Dancers

In his research, Abraham Maslow found that people who trust their instincts are more creative and have more "peak experiences." During these experiences, a person feels juiced, confident, and on a roll. That's what a quarterback feels when he gracefully launches the ball to a distant receiver on the run. It's what a dancer feels when, instead of moving, he feels he is being moved.

Maslow said that such experiences are available to the rest of us driving to work, cutting the grass, talking with friends. The requirement for having a peak experience is that we trust our impulses. In other words, if I am a squirrel, I should delight in running and climbing no matter who tells me my place is in the water.

Of course, I think it's important to recall that quarterbacks and artists, though centered, get weary. While our true path includes doing what feels good, there is a bit more to it than that. Life includes more than just peak experiences.

Meaningful But Not Always Thrilling

I once attended a meeting for caregivers of disabled people, and in the group was a mother of a twenty-six-year-old schizophrenic son. She captured everyone's attention by a genuine peace in the face of her burden. Someone asked how she managed, and she said, "I don't know. I always try to remember what my mother said: 'If it falls to you, do it.'" You could tell by her face that "Do it" meant really do it, without martyrdom or resentment but accepting what could not be given to anyone else.

Because this lady remained opened rather than closed, she experienced a depth of meaning that is rare. She was pretty adept at maintaining openness because her mother was such a good model. And I suppose she sometimes lost that openness as all real people do. Great artists and inventors go through dry periods, and saints get lost in their dark night of the soul. So if we ourselves hit the snooze alarm faced with decisions that seem too heavy, it doesn't mean we are off the path. And, by the way, we're in good company.

Signs of Life in Strange Places

In his book *At An Intensive Journal Workshop,* Progoff tells about an archeological dig in the nineteenth century during which part of a tree was found in a three-thousand-year-old tomb. A seed was embedded in the wood and someone planted it out of curiosity. Much to the scientist's surprise, the seed began to grow. It missed its chance in ancient Egypt, but three thousand years later it sprang to life.

Often we feel that opportunities missed early on are now out of reach, that what we wished we could have done, experienced, felt, will never again be available. But if we stay open in light of what we now know, we may breathe life into what appears to be skimpy material. Perhaps your dream was buried under criticism, shame, or the dismissive attitudes of others, and you dosed the fire of your passion. You can rekindle it by "parenting" yourself now.

Is It Really Never Too Late?

Someone said that it's never too late to be what you always wanted to be, and I suspect there's at least an element of truth in that. Ask yourself what you haven't asked since childhood: What do I want to be when I grow up? What longing is still there that over the years has been silenced? Perhaps you won't revive the original dream, but you might live it in another form. So you couldn't study music as a child. How have you put music into your life? So you couldn't go to medical school. What have you done with your need for healing and caring? Whatever your longing, tend to it, talk about it, read about it, dream it, and no matter how slight a thing you do, live it.

A Tip-off from a Sore Back

We all indulge in the "If I had it to do all over again, what would I do" game. Maybe I would be just what I am. However, I wouldn't be surprised if I didn't move more toward my too-dormant passions for photography, music, writing, and other arts that in the past I dared not think of. Once my friend Joanna, who plays the piano, called and said she had bought some new sheet music and invited my wife and me over for coffee with her and her husband Tony. She and I played four hands together, with emphasis on "playing," as we laughed at mistakes that came mostly from my terrible sight-reading. Later that evening as we left, I noticed that I didn't have the backache I had when we first arrived, and I wondered what I had done to my health by neglecting my love of music. I also wondered what else I had done by repressing so much of that playful, poetic, imaginative side of myself. Within a month, I had bought a grand piano and resumed the piano lessons that came to a screeching halt when I became a "responsible" adult. Eventually I stopped those lessons again, and the instrument often stands there neglected, but it stands as a reminder of my wholeness and that special place of life and energy within myself.

Part of the core of this book and, I believe, of our lives, is some kind of frequent return to that place. Whatever we do, whether running a business, making love, or tossing a ball, all are pulled together and draw meaning from that nucleus. It becomes for us, then, home base, the centerpiece and touchstone of our lives.

Practice this—

> Go to a quiet place with something to write on and imagine that you are a child. Take your time and allow yourself to feel as if you are once again unaware of how much it might cost to go to school, how difficult it might be, how inappropriate it might be, and begin writing "When I grow up I want to..." and let your imagination fly. Disregard the voices that say how silly or crazy you are for thinking this way and keep writing for at least fifteen minutes. Use your imagination not only to create pictures but to create excitement within yourself. You don't have to worry about being in denial if you say you are deliberately playacting. When you finish, ask yourself if what you have written is really such a bad idea. Or, if the scene as a whole is out of the question, in what smaller ways can you begin to live what you may have been ignoring?

CHAPTER 5

Opening the Sluice

Imagine that all we need to live fulfilling lives is constantly flowing from our source as water flows through a passageway. Right now, that source is showing us how to find our life's work, how to tend our garden, or how to work through a disagreement with a friend. Spiritual traditions have often described that source as a spring, a river, or a well, providing us with life's essential nutrients. Everyone who has used those analogies says that while we don't generate the source, we do control the flow. The handle that opens and closes the valve is in our hands.

A client who was a lover of words pictured the process as opening and closing a sluice. A sluice is a trough for conveying water. It has a valve that either holds the water back or lets it flow. Similarly, we can either allow or disallow the flow from our source by opening or closing our personal valves. Because we unconsciously turn the valve one way or the other, it is important to know when this is happening and how to consciously reopen the valve when it is closed.

Open or Closed

Judy had been offered a new job as an office manager. She was excited about a fresh start and glad to leave a company where she worked for an employer who was constantly disgruntled. Also she was proud that this opportunity came because of her reputation and that she was already assured of the position. Moving out of the old place and into the new environment was exhilarating, and her mind clicked confidently with plans to reorganize the new office.

A week before she was to begin her job, she received a call telling her of an interview she was to have with her new employer. The interview was just a formality. Up until this point, her valve had been wide open. When she hung up the phone, though, she suddenly thought, "What if I say the wrong thing while talking to my new boss? What if I come across as stupid?" The thoughts went on, "I've quit my old job. What will happen if he doesn't hire me?" Before long, she had visions of herself in a soup line at the local shelter for the homeless, and her valve was closed tight. Then she developed a tension headache, and it seemed that everything she did for the rest of the day went sour.

Judy began closing her valve when she stopped thinking about what she wanted to do and began thinking about what she didn't want. When she closed down, she lost her direction because she shifted into worry mode—considering only negative possibilities instead of the ones she wanted.

The good news is that we can shift to an open state when we think about what we do want. I like to think of this as being open not only to the surface wishes of our egos but also open to what we want at our deepest level, which includes all that our source is giving us. This is the attitude psychologist Carl Rogers describes as "openness to experience" or being free of preoccupation with the past and the future. While in that state, in addition to concentrating on what we want, we are open to all potential.

Like Judy, we can feel the difference when we are opened or closed. When our valve is open, our bodies and minds feel flexible, free, and hopeful. When closed, we feel constricted, stuck, cynical, and defensive. An open attitude spurs our creativity because we are thinking outside the pebble where there are more options, and we are free to experiment. Just as things went continually wrong when Judy's valve was closed, when it was open, she had the opposite experience of being on a roll with things going repeatedly right.

What Golfers Show Us

In addition to an open valve, I also like to refer to that state as having an open stance. By "stance" I mean not only that short warm up and positioning an athlete goes through prior to moving into action but also an attitude he takes with him through the game. For a golfer, his stance within that few seconds of quiet stillness just before the swing is loaded with conscious and unconscious feelings that set the course of the ball. An expert can tell just where the ball will fly by observing the position of the golfer's feet, hands, or head. Often you don't have to be an expert to tell whether the shot will be a good or a bad one. If a person's brow is wrinkled tight, the jaw set hard, the shoulders pulled up with determination, the golfer is likely thinking, "This is difficult. I don't know if I can do it." That closed stance leads to a bad shot and a bag of clubs in the lake. When the stance is relaxed, the eyes calmly focused, the golfer is likely thinking, "I can do this. I need to concentrate, but it's fun." That open stance paves the way for the hit to be solid and the ball to go in the intended direction. For our purpose, that stance is something the golfer has not only in the tee box but also while walking the fairway. We have either an open or closed stance right now, and that stance will largely determine the rest of our day or night. If you happen to find your stance is closed, here's how to open it.

The Positive Use of Life's Bumps

Since Judy learned what she was unconsciously doing to close her valve, she is able to keep it open for longer periods of time. She does this by recognizing what she is thinking and redirecting her thoughts. When she finds herself focusing on what she doesn't want, she deliberately chooses to think about what she does want until she begins to feel good. She is making a habit of this practice so that it becomes just as second nature to her as worry once was.

Author and motivational speaker Esther Hicks has compared this redirecting to correcting our path while driving the freeway. If we veer too far left or right, we feel little bumps under our tires that tell us we are moving out of our lane. When that happens, we don't get desperate or irritated that we are headed in the wrong direction. Rather, we use those bumps as signals to get back on course. We can do the same thing when we notice distress in our lives and, thus, avoid getting hooked on the worry-go-round. Sometimes it's relatively easy to do this. You have a flat tire, and you notice your body tightening as you begin to recall that your warranty just ran out and how upset your co-workers will be because you will be late for the meeting. As these depressing thoughts begin to mount, you foresee the destruction of the rest of your day. But then you take a deep breath and ask yourself what you want, given the circumstances. You want the flat to be fixed, so you can get to your meeting. You want to stay calm. You want to feel good about yourself even if people are upset that you are late. As you focus on things turning out well, your almost boiling blood lowers to a simmer, and you gradually cool off. You can practice these "quickies" while you continue what you are doing.

When I do that, I not only feel better, but often things take a positive turn in ways for which I have no explanation. Perhaps my experiencing of the universe's interconnectedness beyond what I can see rests upon my openness. If that is so, my openness to experience, even when stressed, is crucial. My tendency to postpone contentment until I get my wish is a recipe for disaster. Too often, I think that I will be happy "when": I get a new job, a new house, finish the report, find the right mate. But what if the resolution of these things is dependent upon my feeling good first?

Psychiatrist Shinoda Bolen, in her book *The Tao of Psychology*, says that tapping into the greater resources beyond the ego comes from "a hopeful expectancy." She says that when we live with that hope, "divine intervention" provides answers when we face difficulties. This divine intervention can take a variety of forms. As Bolen puts it, "A creative solution may emerge from within our minds, an amazing synchronicity may occur that solves the situation, or a dream may provide direction or the answer may come in meditation."

When It Takes Longer

These "quickies" work to get us through life's everyday stresses and disappointments, but in other circumstances, it may be next to impossible to redirect our thinking quickly. When overwhelmed by responsibilities or faced with physical pain, our thoughts may be so scrambled and our nervous system so tight that we may need to do something more radical to encourage a shift in our stance.

Clay identified himself as a negative thinker, saying that his motto was "If it weren't for bad luck, I'd have no luck at all." We talked about practicing "openness to experience," and he decided to practice redirecting and keeping his valve open. When he returned the following week, he said it didn't work, and he gave up after three or four tries. I asked him to tell me about his attempts, and he told me that the first time he tried was when he and his wife had to rush their child to the emergency room. The next time was after an exhausting day's work when he checked the mail and learned his taxes were to be audited. The other times were of equal weight and shock, and all he could do with any of them was to hang on while he went into his usual tailspin.

I suggested two things to Clay. First, during the coming week, he should practice with events that did not have such emotional importance, so that when the more significant problems arose he would be able to apply what he had practiced on those. Secondly, I suggested that for these bigger problems, when possible, he stop what he was doing and write about how he wanted to feel and how he wanted his life to go until he felt good. The second suggestion was the hardest to follow because his mind was more at home thinking of how awful things were. He found it hard to stop what he was doing and take more than a short pause. He began to force himself to walk, talk to friends, or watch his favorite movies so that the tension could drain from his taut body and mind before he tackled the challenge before him. As he practiced this, he began to get the knack of it and gradually came to know that he need not be a victim of his moods.

A Way of Life

We will talk more later about working through change and how some changes require an extended process of reassessing our values, deciding to let some go and integrate new ones. But no matter how long it takes, we are still working with the same principle of opening to the present moment and honestly being ourselves. That ever-recurring process of opening and closing is part of the "stuff of life" we mentioned in the last chapter and is as natural as eating, getting hungry, and filling up again. For me, the reopening we are talking about gives practical meaning to two ancient concepts, forgiveness and love. When I am open, in the present, not binding myself, another person, or the world by my small ego thoughts, I am practicing love in its highest sense. Forgiveness is getting back to that state when we have lost it.

If you find the practice of staying open difficult to sustain, you needn't feel alone because some of the world's great thinkers have wrestled with this issue. In the next chapter, we will talk about some of the advice those thinkers have passed on about maintaining openness.

Practice this—

> Think of something you are trying to accomplish. Sit alone and write without stopping to think of how you want things to turn out. Include how you want to feel, the details of what the finished product will look like, and how favorably others will react to what you have done. Include that you are open to all possible ways for your project to be completed, saying things like "It is satisfying to know that there are so many possibilities," or "I trust that one or more of the many possible ways for this to be complete has begun to happen." If you feel ridiculous, don't let that stop you. In fact, you might expect to feel ridiculous if this kind of thinking is very different for you. Write until you feel good, and then read what you have written. Keep it within your reach, and read it at least once a day or whenever you need to. Whenever you find yourself closing down, recall what you have written until you feel good.

CHAPTER 6

If You Don't Meditate, Moodle

J ung says something that rings true for me: Consciousness resists
anything unconscious. In other words, we would be more creative if we were not so afraid of the dark. Even though we may
accept that keeping our valve open to the greater resources within and
around us is the path to fulfillment, we fear doing so.

The *Course in Miracles* puts it strikingly when it says that while
putting the ego's view of the world aside to allow for something greater
is a release from hell, the ego sees it as a descent into hell. No wonder
the simple openness suggested in the last chapter is often so difficult.
With one hand, we embrace change and transformation, and with the
other, we resist them. Some of the world's oldest practices were de-
vised to address this issue. These techniques reduce the anxiety of
opening to greater possibilities as well as help us to see openness as an
advantage. I am going to talk about meditation, one of my favorite
ways of doing that and suggest a few others.

Still Waters

There is an ancient adage that says, "When muddy water is allowed to become still, it becomes clear. When it becomes clear, it re-

flects its depth." Our minds are like water that under the influence of activity and stress become cloudy so that we can't see clearly. Meditation is one way to allow the waters to settle. I don't believe everyone has to meditate, but I am convinced that everyone must find his own way to let the waters settle, so new things can arise for our safe consideration.

How to Be Productive by Doing Nothing

Tension aggravates pain, and relaxation alleviates it. To emphasize the importance of relaxing when a person experiences pain, I once told a pain management class about letting the waters settle. The next week, one of the participants presented me with a wonderful gift and tool for "show and tell" meditation. I was touched that she was giving me her own handmade souvenir, a small jar containing water from the White River in South Dakota. When she gently handed it to me, the water was crystal clear, but the more we handled it, sediment from the bottom was disturbed, clouding the water. When the jar was shaken, it was impossible to see anything except darkness. Often when talking about learning to be still to clarify the mind, I will shake the jar and hand it to a client and ask him to clear the water. Some people see the obvious, put the jar down, and let nature take its course. Others fall prey to our tendency to complicate things. They wonder what to *do* with the jar. The obvious answer—that we do nothing with it—is often what we need to do to manage our troubled minds. Physician Larry Dossey calls meditation the gentle art of doing nothing and claims that three-fourths of all headaches can be cured by doing nothing. What else might we be able to accomplish by this kind of doing nothing?

How I Started Doing Nothing

In the sixties, Transcendental Meditation became popular partly under the influence of notables like the Beatles. Transcendental meditation is a form of mantra meditation, the mental repetition of a pleasant-sounding word. Actually, rather than doing nothing, it is narrowing one's focus to the least possible thing to do, a sort of putting the mind's gears in idle or neutral. This turns off the rational mind as we let go of the effort to fix things, make life different, or figure life out. We then experience a very calming effect, which clarifies thinking once thinking is resumed.

When word of the benefits of meditation caught the attention of cardiologist Dr. Herbert Benson, he took the technique into the research lab. There he attached meditating medical students to machinery that peered into their hidden physiology and told him what was going on when one sat and did what appeared to be nothing. Dr. Benson found a range of important physical changes that influence our health, including lowered blood pressure, decreased brain wave activity, lower rates of metabolism, and fewer stress hormones in the blood stream. He called the state we reach when all this happens the "relaxation response." It is the opposite of the hyped state we call the "flight or fight" response.

After Benson published his first book, *The Relaxation Response,* a friend told me of his own experience while meditating and what a great stress reducer it was for him. That caught my interest because of symptoms I had that I knew were aggravated by stress, not the least of which was insomnia. Often I unwillingly witnessed the sunrise. I learned the technique and looked forward to doing something so important that required I not try hard. I took to it easily because it appealed to my reclusive nature, giving me reason to be alone. (I had another friend, though, who also liked doing it from the start, and he is an extroverted chatterbox.) I meditated twice a day for twenty minutes, once in the morning and once before supper and was soon hooked on a routine that I still keep. There was no question that the practice reduced my stress. Within two weeks, I began to fall into deeper sleep and slept through the night. Even now, if I have difficulty sleeping, it is usually when I shorten my meditation or fail to do it in the evening.

The Bonus

After meditating for a few weeks, I found that stress reduction was not the only benefit of meditation. For the first time, I saw what the Eastern adage "emptiness refills itself" meant. As I practiced letting go, I saw problems in a new light after I finished. Problems didn't vanish, but they were not as heavy and seemed more manageable. It was like the experience of "sleeping on" a problem. Things I had heard all my life in my own tradition began to make sense: "Unless the seed falls to the ground it will not bear fruit." Unless I practice letting go of what my ego holds as sacred, my efforts to be creative will not work. I began to appreciate how letting go, at least temporarily, can be an advantage. Detachment, preached to me all my life, lost its distaste because I began to see detachment as a way to open the valve behind which lay the fullest possible expression of my talents and potential. Because of that, I experienced what so many others struggle to explain about meditation, that it is a way of "coming home." In his book *How to Meditate,* psychologist Lawrence Le Shan says, "We meditate to find, to recover, to come back to something of ourselves we once dimly and unknowingly had and have lost without knowing what it was or where or when we lost it."

I developed what psychiatrist Dr. William Glasser calls a "positive addiction" to meditation. But it never became completely easy, and it is not now. I continue doing it because, for me, it works. Sometimes I'd rather not meditate, and sometimes when I do, I'm distracted or bored. When that happens, I remind myself of the beneficial changes that occur if I stick with it, changes I can't see but Dr. Benson's smart machines can. I recall that letting go sets into motion adjustments in my physiology that I can't begin to will, and my motivation increases. I am then reminded of the psychological counterpart of that principle. Jung says, "We must be willing to let things happen in the psyche," implying that our source knows how to transform us if we sometimes take our hands off. Meditation is for me one of the best ways I know for taking my hands off so that the part of my psyche that works beneath the surface is free to do its reorganizing.

The Underground Stream

Many say that during meditation they feel a oneness with others and the rest of the universe. I have never had a blinding realization of that during meditation. Often I feel a great peace, clarity, and the experience of having, for the moment, come home. But I can't say that while I meditate I feel a greater connection to you, my family, my cat, or dog.

However, while I might not feel that connection during meditation, I definitely sense common bonds as I go about my business. During meditation, I allow worries and prejudices about myself and the rest of the world to fall away. When that happens, I am more comfortable with myself and thus with everyone else. Because I am less guarded, I see ties with others that surprise me. I even see undeniable ties with those I prefer to claim no relation. I get glimpses of how I am cut from the same fabric, have the same tendencies, the same fears.

How Do You Let the Waters Settle?

Just as there are many different ways to meditate, there are many different ways besides meditation to let the muddy waters settle. I don't think all of these ways have been taken into Dr. Benson's research lab, but if we pay attention, common sense tells us they work to open us to possibilities. For instance, I often find myself walking wet from the shower to my journal because of a comment my wife once made. One morning, when I came out of the shower saying, "Do you know what I'm going to do?" she said that she was going to buy me a waterproof recorder because I so frequently finished my shower with "Do you know what I'm going to do?" Since her comment, that steamy chamber has become one of my best idea places, something I didn't know until she brought it to my attention. New ideas crop up because the hot water that melts tension in my muscles also loosens the death clutch I have on thoughts. Walking on the beach, listening to music, dancing, and, if we let it, just sitting around doing nothing in particular can slow the mind's machinery to idle and thus stimulate new awarenesses.

The Benefits of Moodling

Brenda Euland in her jewel of a book *If You Want to Write,* says that the imagination needs occasions when we are "idle, limp and alone for much of the time, as lazy as men fishing on a levee." She has an interesting name for this inactivity, which I can't find in the dictionary. She defines "moodling" as "long, inefficient, happy idling, dawdling and puttering."

Unfortunately, when we need this time the most, we often have a firewall between ourselves and any kind of moodling. I think we sometimes say "the more stress the better," not even knowing that the waters have become muddy, and as tension mounts, we keep moving through the fog as if we know what we are doing.

The objection to resting or shifting the mind into idle is that we will waste time and grow lazy. But the pause we reluctantly take will make us more efficient and responsible because however we do it, through meditation, walks, or moodling, in that pause we will find a spring of creativity and renewal. Once there, we can see what we normally don't see. The project we are working on or the issue we worry about will be seen differently, like the detail in a painting that is impossible to see as long as the artist has his nose against the canvas. And during that pause, other neglected questions can be addressed: Who am I? Where is my life going? What means the most to me?

On to the Olympics

Ultimately, openness is not a technique or an exercise but an attitude that allows our best and truest selves to come out. During the winter Olympics I learned that many of the athletes work with sports psychologists. These athletes were taught to frequently practice deep relaxation during which they imagined themselves giving the performance of their lives, feeling the experience deeply within. They then consciously maintained that focus throughout the real performance. That kind of practice leads to a state of openness to experience, relaxed attention, freedom, and a healthy recklessness.

The ideal example of this came from gold medalist Sara Hughes, a picture of happy grace and precision, who said she hit the ice telling herself she wanted to have a good time. She was not the favorite, had no title to defend, reminded herself that she had nothing to lose, and won the gold. I don't know if she worked with a sports psychologist—and almost found myself doing research to find out if she did—but that would be missing the point. The point is her attitude, however she acquired it. And the point for us is that we shoot for her openness to life and her nothing-to-lose style even under tough circumstances. For most of us, especially those of us who have lived long enough to doubt our mind's natural ability, we may need to practice. That's what the last two chapters have been about.

Practice this—

1. Using the following guidelines, meditate once or twice a day for two weeks or more and then decide if you want to continue doing so.

    •   Choose a pleasant sounding word or phrase. Some people like to use a word that has no meaning, or as little meaning as possible so that it does not stimulate thoughts. Dr. Benson suggests using the word "one" if it appeals to you. Other possibilities are "peace," "shalom," "center," "all," or phrases like "be still," "slow down," or any other word or short phrase.

    •   Sit where you will not be disturbed and close your eyes. For one minute, do nothing except notice your surroundings. Notice your body against whatever you are sitting on. Notice any sounds you hear or thoughts that come to mind. Do nothing with any of these things except observe them.

    •   After one minute begin to repeat your word mentally, almost as if you are hearing it slowly. Some like to repeat the word with each exhalation of breath. When you are distracted by other thoughts, sounds, feelings, rather than try to put those out of your mind, notice them and calmly turn your attention back to your word. If you handle distractions this way, they do not interfere, no matter how many times they occur.

- It will help you to be patient if you remember that your mind is like the muddy water that clears only over time. Continue in this way for twenty minutes. It's okay to peek at a clock.

- After twenty minutes, discontinue the word but keep your eyes closed and remain still for another two minutes before opening them slowly. You may want to stretch a bit before standing up. Make no judgment about how well you did or did not do. Just notice what the experience felt like and look forward to doing it the next time. Did you feel light, calm, jittery, restless? Whatever the experience, suspend your judgment and let it go for that time.

2. Here is another way to reach a deep state of relaxation and openness.

- Sit down, close your eyes, and at first do nothing except notice whatever comes into your consciousness. Notice any sounds, the temperature of the room, any thoughts, with no intention to do anything with any of these except observe them. Notice your breathing in that way, reminding yourself that you are inhaling energy and exhaling tension.

- Turn your attention to one part of your body at a time, imagining each part of your body relaxing. Rather than try to will yourself to relax, which may make you tenser, in your imagination see and feel tension dissolving in your body. Start with your feet and imagine them relaxing and loosening for a few seconds. If the relaxation does not occur, go to your calves and imagine they are relaxing slowly, and if you are distracted by other thoughts or sounds, don't fight them. Simply turn your attention back to relaxing one part of your body at a time, remembering how the muddy water clears slowly and certainly when you leave it alone.

- Continue with your thighs, pelvic area and hips, hands, the joints of your hands and fingers, slowly up your arms, shoulders and back, neck, the area behind your tongue, the hinge of your jaw, and the rest of your head. Continue to passively disregard distractions, bringing your attention slowly back to relaxing, easily, effortlessly.

- After you have covered each part of your body, slowly count back from ten to zero, saying to yourself, "More relaxed." Then remain as you are for the next few minutes or as long as you are comfortable. Notice what your experience was like, but do not make good or bad judgments about it. Look forward to doing it the next time.

Following these guidelines, you can reach a state of profound relaxation while remaining fully alert. I like to think of that state as an island of time where there is no past to think about and no future to think about. No time is more important than that present moment as you become more and more familiar with the peace that is reached not by pushing and striving but by letting go. You can begin to slowly say the words to yourself, "Letting go, letting go, letting go" as the words take you deeper and deeper to that place that is beyond doubt, argument, or analysis, the place where you are restored, to start again.

CHAPTER 7

The Magic of a Good Ear

"Tell me more; I want to hear it all," Obi Wan Kenobi says to me as I write. Sometimes, it's Einstein who talks to me. Brenda Euland advises authors to write for a person who gives the writer their undivided attention, saying, "Tell me more; I want to hear it all." She says that if writers don't know such a person, then they should make one up. I know people who will do that for me, but they're not always around, so sometimes I make someone up or "borrow" someone from history. The effect of such regard from another is often surprising, priming inspiration that otherwise would not have occurred.

Psychologist Carl Rogers recognized how transforming listening could be and built a whole system of counseling on it. He believed that what we need for wholeness is within us and that when someone listens, free of judgment, advice, or interpretation, solutions emerge. He observed that acceptance creates a healthy ecosystem that triggers a chain of growth. Safety leads to freedom, freedom to expression, expression to creativity. That's why in the presence of such a person we find ourselves saying what we didn't think we knew or we move on after a long standstill.

I suspect that we will never outgrow our need for others to listen to us. I also suspect that without the ability to listen to ourselves, the loving acceptance of others will not help. Without a base of internal acceptance, the support of others sustains us only as long as they are around. So we will talk now about how to listen to ourselves, how to provide the safe environment that allows for the fullest expression of our thoughts and talents.

The Mind's Recorder

To begin with, while not aware of it, we are always listening to ourselves. If we're old enough to read this book, we have stored on the recorder of our minds countless opinions and beliefs gathered from past experience. Daily, every minute, the recorder plays them back, and they strongly influence our feelings and behavior. The problem is that some of those opinions and beliefs work for us and some don't. Some are supportive while others make us miserable. Deliberate and conscious listening can help us know if we are living by beliefs that are in our best interest.

We wouldn't have to bother with this so much had we been taught from infancy to discern our own truth from another's opinion. Then when we were children, if someone gave us the impression that we were inadequate, we simply could have said, "Well, that doesn't match the way I feel." There would be nothing recorded for future reference that says, "I'm inadequate" when raising our children, choosing a career, or learning a difficult subject. It's hard to conceive of a world without learned beliefs, though one of the Beatles took a stab at it.

Imagine

For me, John Lennon's song *Imagine* conjures a walk through a world where every experience is new because I haven't yet learned to filter everything through past experience. When I see a sunset, I'm not beset by global warming. When I talk with a person unlike my-self, I'm not poisoned with hatred. When I sit down to eat, I don't fret over which diet is best. And when I observe the ideas that come out of me, I don't distrust them because they don't meet certain standards. Everything is fresh, ready to enjoy, including my own thoughts. The downside to this kind of world is that without some reference to past experience, we will soon get into trouble. There are plenty of environ-mental threats and bad ideas out there, and some standards are neces-sary. So we are happier if we learn from the past. But if in learning, we also come to distrust ourselves, we will be less productive and less serviceable. I'm reminded of Charles, a very competent lab technician who has fought anxiety for most of his life.

Changing Stations

Charles once told me that as a small child if he spilt milk at the table, his father equated that mistake with burning the house down, and his father was not kind. Charles' anxiety as an adult came from an inability to tolerate less than perfection in an imperfect world. He is hardest on himself. Listening to himself is almost impossible because he is blocked by his need to defer to others. If you think we've come to the part of this book where we blame our parents, we haven't. The reason for our behaviors is not always clear, and sometimes emotions are greatly affected by chemical imbalances. But so much of the time behavior is conditioned by our past, causing us to listen not to our deepest selves but to our fears. Charles' behavior was likely a combi-nation of both chemistry and learned behavior. He realized this and used both medication and psychotherapy in his healing.

One behavioral technique he used was what we came to call

changing stations. It is based on two assumptions. First, we are always, at least unconsciously, listening to something recorded from the past that adds greatly to our feelings. Secondly, if what we are listening to does not help us, we can turn our attention to something else that does. This is like changing stations on a radio. When Charles began heading in the direction of uncontrollable anxiety, he would try to become aware of who or what he was listening to. If the voice from inside was unkind, unreasonable, or otherwise destructive, he would "change the station." Doing this worked for him and still does.

The process was not magical for Charles because he had to work at it. But he didn't mind the work because, even though slow, it paid off. He did not deny feeling rotten, which would have made him feel worse. Nor did he attempt to chase his thoughts away, which would have caused them to hang around longer. When he changed stations, he was making a choice for what he judged was best for him.

Rattlesnakes

I think it's important to know just how often and how subtly we listen to stations that don't contribute to the lives we want to lead. Because of an incident that happened to my friend, I call this "creating rattlesnakes." Michael is a very competent and intelligent person who damns the day computers were invented. Reluctantly, he ordered a computer. When it arrived and he opened the box, he said that the thing may as well have been a rattlesnake, given the wave of anxiety that passed over him. Here is a bright man, a gifted, experienced therapist, and station F-E-A-R came through loud and clear, bringing him to his knees. There was no rattlesnake, but listening to the wrong station created one. Another station might have said, "Look, high tech is not your forte, but just take your time; learn to push the right buttons, and you'll be fine." It helps me personally to know how often I listen to the wrong station, and that there are better stations on the dial.

There are countless instances throughout the day when we can either create a rattlesnake or keep our composure. When our plans are interrupted, when we're put on hold, when we're misunderstood—all these are instances during which we can feel overwhelmed, but less so if we learn to change the station. Often when we need to use this concept the most, it is most difficult to do. That's because in situations that irritate us greatly, nerves fire and hormones flood our systems before we can think to move the dial. So it's a good idea to practice changing the station after we meditate or when we are in a calm environment. In those environments, creative stations are easier to find. That's why in the movie *Il Postino,* the poet Pablo Neruda gives the lead character, Marco, the advice he does.

Resting the Mouth and Opening the Ears

Marco, to win the heart of the most beautiful woman in the village, wants to write poetry like Pablo Neruda. When he asks Neruda where metaphors come from, the poet suggests a form of "moodling." He recommends, "Try and walk slowly along the shore as far as the bay and look around." He said that if Marco did that, the metaphors would certainly come. Neruda's suggestion, though not always easy to follow, is a way to listen to ourselves, and, if need be, change the station. While Marco used idle time to listen for metaphors, we can use it to gain clarity on other issues. What is my restlessness about? In a day cramped with plans and responsibilities, what is most important? How do I move past this dead end? Where do I stand in this relationship? These are the kinds of questions that beg us to rest our mouths and open our ears.

Hard Advice

To finish this chapter I am following Neruda's advice by spending a weekend at the beach. When I hit a brick wall, I often get past it by leaving what I am doing and taking a beach walk. At first I still hear the voices that tell me I should grit my teeth and press on at my writing post. I hear "You'd better get back to the house or the weekend will have passed, and you'll have nothing to show for it." But if I slow down and allow myself to be present to the ocean, I understand what Neruda is talking about. Some kind of realignment takes place that I can't reason myself into, and I see the work I had begun in a fresh way and, if you will, hear new things.

Most of us are not so fortunate as to have the ocean in our front yards as I do during this weekend. But we can take our concerns for the same kind of slow walk elsewhere. Or we can bring a problem to a favorite quiet spot. Sometimes it seems the ideas will never come. But if we keep moving, or sitting, eventually our confusion will lift, and we get the answers we need. The hardest part for me is honoring the necessary pace. I want things to move faster, and when they don't, I grow impatient and listening halts.

Listening on the Move

The listening we do when we meditate or get away from it all can prepare us for a kind of fine tuning we can do while active. When you paint a house or make your child's jelly sandwich, you have the same option of really hearing yourself as at the beach. While Neruda advises us to seek out the tranquility of nature, the monk and writer Thich Nhat Hahn, in his book *Peace is Every Step,* shows that peace and productivity are not always dependent on geography. Rather, peace and productivity arise from our being truly present. The trick is to focus on what we hear, see, and feel now, without dwelling on things being otherwise. His book teaches mindfulness, the practice of being totally present, so that we are not "tossed about mindlessly like a bottle slapped here and there on the waves." This enlivens our senses so that we not only hear more but also see, feel, taste, and smell more acutely. The hard part is to continue doing that when things don't go the way we want them to go. The following are examples of how I stop listening and lapse into mindlessness and how I'm learning to do it differently. I use these examples because most of our days are filled with similar frustrations and practicing with them can strengthen us for more critical times.

How a Derailed Door Derailed My Life

One night recently while straightening the house after a visit from our two-year-old grandson, I noticed a sliding closet door off its tracks. I knew the door was easy to replace, but when I picked it up and put the little wheels on their tracks, they came off and the door clunked to the floor. I replaced the door and it fell again. I didn't like that because it was late, and I was ready for sleep. I squeezed into the closet to get a better view of things, hung the door again, and it fell off again. When it fell after another try, I vowed that if it took me until sunrise, I would reposition that door. After a few more attempts, I screamed at it, jiggled it, and hit it hard. Breathing heavily and clenching my teeth, I could see where this was going, especially when I saw the little stabilizer on the floor splintered. I admitted defeat and decided that when the carpenter came to fix the garage door, he would know what to do, and I went to bed.

Awakened by the clock radio the next morning, my mind went immediately to the door tracks. In that rested state, I saw the solution clearly. Somehow the inner and outer sliding doors had gotten reversed, something I couldn't see in my tired and frustrated state. I went immediately to the closet, reversed the doors and hung them. Throughout the day, I kept thinking about how *certain* I was about the workings of those doors, how justified my anger was, and how wrong I was. I also thought about how easily that same "certainty" could make me miserable over more important issues, such as my work, my impression of others, my health.

Saran Wrap™

Did you ever angrily toss Saran Wrap™ into the garbage can because it was rolled tight and you couldn't find its end? I was about to do that when I felt the presence of that Vietnamese monk who said, "Just be patient. Completely relax and take your time. Now that you're really relaxed, imagine you are listening, and move the tube slowly in your hands, noticing everything you feel." "Ah ha," I said, "there's the end of the wrap." The rest was easy.

I suggested this approach to a client who later told me it also works great with tangled extension chords and monofilament fishing line. We talked about how different life would be if we applied the same principle to our sometimes impossibly tangled lives. When we see no exit from financial knots or pressing decisions about our work, can we relax into the present, hold our lives like that tube, and move slowly to discover what we would normally miss?

Choosing to be Present

I remember our teacher in elementary school sitting at her desk checking the roll. As she called our names we said, "Present." Really, though, we were on the ball field, at a movie, running through our neighborhoods, anything but present. Frequently we are anything but present to life, but the good news is that listening to ourselves can wake us up and bring us back.

Often listening is simply choosing to be attentive to what is really going on while we trust our hunches and try out ideas. It is also listening to others and being fully present to them, something that is easier to do when we are aware of our own inner voices. Listening is creating mini-vacations as we sometimes drive with the radio or CD player turned off, the easier to view our inner landscape and sort things out. Time allowing, it is driving the long way to our destination through a pleasant neighborhood. We could really get radical and take advantage of the slow traffic instead of cursing it. You may be surprised at what simple changes like these can make over just a few days. If you have a worrisome problem, try one of them for a week or so. It will help if, instead of fully developed momentous answers, you look for hunches and inklings. Most important answers have those kinds of small beginnings, but if we don't trust them, they lead nowhere. Trusting our own ideas, even when they're not earth shattering, revs our creativity. Expecting that we will hear the secret the world has been waiting for will frustrate us. This was highlighted to a client in an amusing way.

There is No Secret

Vincent, a forty-seven-year-old high school math teacher, originally came to therapy because he was ambivalent about his career. It didn't take long for him to know, however, that if he could get past feeling burned out and make his work more interesting, he preferred to remain teaching for the long haul. An idea that Vincent trusted and used often was to record his counseling sessions and listen to the tapes during the week. One day, he fastened his seatbelt, turned on the engine, and reached for the stash of tapes he kept in a box. He noticed one labeled, "The Secret," and put it in the tape deck. No sound. He turned up the volume. No sound. He fast-forwarded. No sound. He turned the tape over. No sound. The tape was blank.

We had a good laugh and, of course, concluded that there is no secret. We also talked about how, if there is a secret, it is to learn to trust and experiment with your own ideas. We recalled how frequently Vincent was put back on track by simple solutions that arose during his counseling, and he would say, "Why didn't I think of that?" Often he had thought of the answer, but he wasn't tuned in because he didn't trust himself. Or he didn't stay tuned in because the message wasn't grand enough.

Testing What You Hear

A realistic view of listening respects that life is like that maze we mentioned earlier and through which we take twists and turns rather than move in a straight line. Clarity from our source often comes like flashes of lightning that never permanently eliminate the dark. Nor do these flashes dispense with our need for discretion and the responsibility to ask whether, in our listening, we heard what is really best or what our impatient and biased egos wanted to hear. Countless wars have been waged by persons who said they heard God tell them to do it. Everything we hear must stand the test of time and take its place with other factors in our lives and the lives of others. A sudden urge to move abroad either to feed the poor or live on the Mediterranean must be balanced against practicalities, responsibilities, and the ongoing process of our lives. We will always ask, "What does it all mean, how does it all fit, what is being asked of me now?" And the psyche will always be a slow cooker, giving us answers over a lifetime.

Listening to the Eskimos

Microbiologist Rene Dubois wrote a book called *A God Within* in which he tells of a moving ritual that Eskimo ivory carvers observed. They first sat in silence and respectfully whispered to the ivory before making a cut, "Who are you? Who lives inside you?" The carver did not presuppose what shape the ivory would take nor did he impose a plan without first seeing the nature of the ivory rooted inside. To live with integrity and purpose, shouldn't we respect our own natural harmony and shape, not assuming in advance that what we see is best? Might we not often sit before the doors of our minds and ask, "Who are you? Who lives inside you?"

Practice this—

Think of something about which you are undecided. It may be whether to change jobs, how to reduce stress in your life, or if you should stay in a relationship. Go where you will not be disturbed and recall the problem in detail. As you think of the problem, notice what it looks like and what it feels like to have it. Then close your eyes, relax, and imagine that the answer you need is somewhere deep within you. Then say to yourself slowly, "What I really need to do is…." See what solution or step toward a solution comes up.

Then continuing to relax, ask yourself if the answer fits. As you do this, see what happens in your body, whether you feel lighter, slightly more energetic or not. If you sense some inner rightness about the answer but an inability to move toward it, repeat the process with your new information. For instance, perhaps the answer to what you really need to do is talk to your boss, but when you check it for rightness, you feel tight in your body because you don't know if you can talk to your boss. Then repeat the process about talking to your boss, starting with "What I really need to do about that is…." Check that for rightness by seeing what your body feels. Keep doing this until you get clearer.

CHAPTER 8

Listening Through Our Fingers

Gaston Bachlard, a French philosopher, made the following statement that darts to something inside me: "The source of our first suffering lies in the fact that we hesitated to speak. It was born in the moment we accumulated silent things within us." Those silent things are what we begin to release when we move closer to that touchstone inside. There we find the feelings that we have been talked out of, the sadness, the bitterness, and the fear, and behind those, we uncover the visions, longings, preferences, and talents that enable us to take our place in the world.

In this chapter, I'm going to introduce you to a friend who can help you begin to release those silent things. But before I introduce you, agree not to skip the chapter when I tell you who your friend is. Agreed? Okay.

The trusted partner I am referring to is your journal. Some of you are cringing, sorry that you made the agreement. You flash back to high school, the pain of essays. But the kind of journal I'm talking about has nothing to do with being a writer or knowing the rules of grammar. In fact, I wonder if you might be more successful with this kind of journal if you are not a good writer. After trying what I suggest, you may decide not to use the practice, but don't make that decision because you are not a creative writer. Also don't decide against the practice because you don't like to write. "I don't like to write" usually means "I hated what I was taught about writing," or "I hated the frown on my teacher's face."

Our Swiss Army Knife™

A journal can be an organizer for confusion, a sleuth for finding lost parts of ourselves, a safe place to explore our feelings, and a repository for our dreams. Some use journals casually, a periodic check to keep life on track. Others feel their journals are essential lifelines to sanity. Author Graham Green says, "Sometimes I wonder how all those who do not write, compose, or paint can manage to escape the madness, the melancholia, the panic fear which is inherent in the human situation." Because a journal is so many tools in one, I think of it as the Swiss Army Knife™ for designing our lives.

Simple Rules

The rules are simple: write non-stop and don't evaluate what you write. When we write non-stop and without evaluation, we may leave in our wake incorrect sentences, misplaced periods, foul language, and embarrassing thoughts. This will be easier if we remember that the practice has nothing to do with being polite or being a good writer. It has everything to do with whether we can stand ourselves without sprucing up our language, diluting our opinions, or mitigating how we feel. Free writing, loose and reckless, is the "style" of choice for this kind of journal. One helpful requirement is that we write for a certain time or a stated number of pages that represents a stretch for us. When I was first introduced to this kind of writing, I was advised to write for at least ten to fifteen minutes daily for a month. Julia Cameron, in her book *The Artist's Way*, suggests we write each morning for three full pages.

That stretch keeps us from stopping when our egos whine that we're not making sense or that we're not getting anywhere. Promise your ego structure at a later date but not while you are writing in your journal, and let her rip.

The Payoff for Writing Through Trash

Most people are amazed by what comes out of their pens or onto the computer screen, and they see the point of Graham Wallas who said, "How do I know what I think 'til I see what I say?" With this kind of writing we enter the heart of creativity. Bill Stott, in his book *Write to the Point and Feel Better about Your Writing*, calls it "unfettered mental play." When we write in this way, we even accept trash because often what looks like trash, coupled with tomorrow's junk, are the seeds of new insights. If we edit too soon because we want to be neat, clean, or intelligible, ideas trying to push to the surface never make it.

Journals in the Lab

Psychologist Dr. James W. Pennebaker has taken journals into the research lab and shown that those who write about their deepest thoughts and feelings not only have better insight but are physically healthier. In his book *Opening Up: the Healing Power of Confiding in Others*, he says that, "Translating our thoughts into language is psychologically and physically beneficial." He studied two groups, those who wrote for twenty minutes a day about anything, and those who wrote for the same length of time their deepest feelings about a traumatic experience. According to blood studies, the group that wrote about their deeper thoughts and feelings had a stronger immune system at the end of the study. Pennebaker also found that this group came to organize and understand thoughts and feelings that would have otherwise remained confusing. That's why those who keep journals speak of them as a trusted friend or confidant who stands by and allows them to talk of the gross in themselves as well as the beautiful, the dark together with the light.

Sticking Around When Things Aren't Pretty

Part of my work as a therapist is in a hospital, counseling cancer patients. It's not uncommon that I have to grab whatever container is in sight and hold it for them while they vomit. They are apologetic, but I always act unruffled. Because I don't run away from their puke, often a special trust is forged over those few minutes.

That's what happens when someone sitting in my office emotionally regurgitates, finally releasing what they consider the ugliest parts of themselves. Likewise, we can learn to be on better terms with ourselves by writing what has been too frightening or embarrassing to face, such as hateful, envious, or jealous thoughts. When we try to ignore them or push them out of consciousness so they won't bother us, they become more damaging. If we accept them to the point of writing them down, they no longer haunt us. Written down, they hurt no one, and our behavior toward ourselves and others is less likely to be hurtful. We are then free to pursue creative choices instead of using our energy to keep demons at bay.

Cutting and Pasting

While in the sanctuary of our journals we can experiment—cut and paste our lives in imagination. For instance, we can try out how to say things we don't ordinarily say and experience what it feels like. I once had a client who found disagreements painful and frightening. In her journal, she practiced confronting a friend about an emotionally charged issue. After actually talking to the person, she felt better—though they disagreed—because she was more comfortable in her own position. I also know people who, after they practiced disagreeing in their journals, dropped the issue because when they saw it written, the issue lost its punch. We can even come to see the other person's point of view and feel fine about it.

In that special place, we can experiment in other ways by freeing our imaginations to move backward or forward in time. We can ask, "What would life be like if I had gone to law school or to cooking school or no school at all and opened my own shop? How will it be if I get that new house, new position, or new friend?"

An Idea Catcher

When you write without censorship, you will be surprised by the wit and insight of ideas and thoughts that pop unbidden into your mind. Maybe you have noticed how this happens when you are just babbling to a friend about something, and you begin to see it in a new light. The added advantage of writing those creative flashes down is that they don't evaporate, leaving us wondering not only what they were but where they went. Stored for safekeeping in the darkness of closed covers, they incubate. When we return to them, they sometimes generate more ideas without much struggle.

Going for Guts

Andrew told me he used to keep a journal, but it was boring and led nowhere. His writing, however, was only a log of what happened in his life and didn't help him surmount problems or live more creatively. When he changed his focus from life's surface to include what he inwardly felt, his journal began to pulse with life and speak to him. Notice the difference.

Andrew's facts: "Today we were told our company was being bought out, and we went to lunch and speculated about whether anyone would be let go. Tom thought most of our department would be let go, but Susan felt the department would simply be reorganized. Someone suggested we talk to Jonathan, our supervisor, but he is away on vacation. Maybe after he rests up from his vacation, we can talk to him."

Andrew's feelings: "When we were told our company was being bought out, I was stunned and terrified. All I could think of was how devastating it would be to lose my job at a time like this. I overate at lunch, as I often do when I'm feeling panicky. I was angry a good part of the afternoon and found it hard to concentrate. I know Jonathan is on vacation, but I almost want to call him. I'll talk to him when he gets back."

Writing in this vein not only relieved him of damned up emotions but told him what was important to him and what to do about it.

Breaking Through Obsessions

Esther, a thirty-nine-year-old cancer patient and mother of small children, wanted very much to stay positive because she believed attitude and health are linked. However, her mind was held captive by a dread of recurrence. She could not rid herself of disturbing thoughts even though she tried working hard, walking, getting lost in TV. We talked about using her journal as a way to face and move through these rapids and, in desperation, she began to write. When "what ifs" came up, rather than push them out of her mind, she paused and answered them as honestly as she could.

"What if the cancer comes back? What if chemo is necessary? What if I can't work? What if I die?" To her surprise, facing and answering questions she had skirted brought her peace even though her circumstances had not changed. She recognized how dodging what is unpleasant had confused her rather than helped, and began to shift from avoiding frightening issues to facing them, the better to move through them. Now with her journal, she does that more easily.

Getting to Know Your Friend

As you get to know your journal better, you will know yourself more deeply because you will be listening more closely to yourself. Your journal will not replace the attention or loving touch of a human friend. However, you may find at times that a friend, no matter how intimate, cannot offer what your journal does. There is a necessary solitude, sometimes referred to as a sacred space by saints and philosophers, inaccessible to anyone but ourselves. Our journals can help lead us to that place and deepen our experience there so that we emerge more creative and serviceable.

Practice this—

Imagine there are no expert writers in the world, just people who sometimes sit and write what they see, think, and feel. With no one to compare yourself to and no legislation to restrain you, find a private place and free write for ten minutes a day, longer if you are comfortable. Do this for a month, writing with and through your feelings, your nonsense, boredom, and embarrassment. Make no decision about whether this is useful for you or not until your month is up.

CHAPTER 9

Creative Darkness

Julia, forty years old, came to me with a bewildering depression. Her feeling was especially disturbing because two years previous she had found relief from the depression that for decades had plagued her. She had assumed it was gone forever. Encouraged and energized, she had learned through seminars, workshops, and books why she was so difficult on herself and how to hold herself in higher esteem. She had made new friends, took up hobbies, and opened her own travel agency. Whatever she touched glowed with success, and her spirits rose high. But in time she noticed that every accomplishment was followed by discontent and emptiness. Instead of satisfaction, she felt boredom, instead of peace, anxiety.

As she spoke of her well-laid plans to keep life intact—her daily reminders of self worth, her meditation sessions, her good eating habits, her disciplined exercise program—and of the emptiness that followed it all, the words of Carl Jung rang in my mind "All excessive purity lacks vitality." Over the next few days, she began to consider its truth. This was the beginning of her release from a self-imposed unconscious prison. Ironically, that release came not because she found more light, gathered more strength and certainty, but because she began to embrace uncertainty. She had been trying to reach some kind of pinnacle, striving to stamp out things about herself she held in contempt—her pain, her fear, her impatience, and other shortcomings. Her efforts had that excessive quality of which Jung spoke, which amounted to painting a picture with no shadows.

Julia's Shadow

Indeed, the name Jung used for that part of Julia she tried so desperately to hide is her shadow. That dark area is the container for what we consider the less perfect parts of ourselves, the parts we keep hidden even from ourselves. As such, it represents the unknown, the unfinished and disorganized aspects of life. The shadow is formed from those personal rules that gain us acceptance or non-acceptance as children. The unacceptable part of ourselves that we learn to ignore, and then to forget, makes up our shadow. Although we avoid our shadow, acceptance of it connects us to a life source because many of our finer impulses and talents are hidden in those recesses. This is sometimes difficult because, as with Julia, most of our culture is not on friendly terms with what is unknown, unfinished, and disorganized. But we pay dearly for making enemies with any part of ourselves.

The Price of Cover-ups

In a thousand ways we deny pain, death, and uncertainty to maintain a pretty front, to be the best looking, the healthiest, the most successful. The "acceptable" person has life in hand, with no worrisome feelings to disturb his or her cool demeanor. If you dance with a Coors™ and smell of Aramis™, you can forget death, disease, hospitals, and funeral homes. In the words of a song by Amanda McBroom called *Growing Up In Hollywood Town*, "Anything you want, you can win, just as long as you're thin, and you never grow old." Our motto might be to keep it right, keep it bright, and colorize our black and white.

But the law of the psyche is that what we disclaim in our lives rules our lives. As the poet Robert Bly says, "Every part of the personality we do not love will become hostile to us." Cover-ups only last for a while before unacknowledged thoughts and feelings erupt in spite of us. They are felt as unexplained anger, depression, defensiveness, or physical symptoms. We see clear examples in public figures, religious leaders, and politicians, whose unconscious impulses force their way to the surface to unmask a self-righteous veneer.

To fit the good-looking mold, we often bury not only weaknesses and flaws, but also talents and traits that define our uniqueness. While we may relegate these qualities to the basements of our minds, they never die—they mutate and turn sour. When we double our efforts to camouflage what we dislike in ourselves, we push what is unwanted back into darkness where it recycles, gathers strength, only to reappear and be more unmanageable than ever. Thus attempts to keep life neat create a mess. No wonder one of our models of the shadow's influence has become *The Strange Story of Dr. Jekyll and Mr. Hyde,* in which a nice man is possessed by a monster.

Reclaiming Ourselves from the Bag

Robert Bly says that our shadow is like a bag of unacceptable traits we began to fill when very young. Since we are unaware of the bag, problems whose origins are in there are worked out on others. After spending years keeping certain traits unconscious, it is disturbing to be reminded of them in someone else. So there is an unconscious urgency to stamp them out, correct them, or banish them. People under our leadership become especially vulnerable to our manipulations. Thus, parents, politicians, doctors, therapists, teachers, and spiritual leaders who never look in the bag use their position to work out unconscious feelings that they project onto others.

Everyone should read what Bly has to say about teaching in his book *The Little Book on the Human Shadow,* and every leader should apply it to his profession. Bly says that a teacher who has claimed her shadow enjoys a natural respect in the classroom even from small children. We cannot help or guide another when we unconsciously dislike or disclaim parts of ourselves. The inner discomfort clouds our vision, makes us tyrannical, or causes us to go limp and back off. Nowhere has this become clearer to me than in my role as a parent.

A Parent's Bag

The issues I have had the most difficulty with as a parent are those that are somehow unfinished in myself. When I am on solid ground, both consciously and unconsciously, I don't waver, and problems are not overwhelming. The "hot" issues, though, have almost driven me to seek out anti-psychotic medication: homework, disorganization, procrastination. About those things, I have had to ask, "What was I doing when I was their age? How organized and prompt am I now?"

My children's academics became less a struggle for me when I was able to show them a report card from my freshman year in high school that reflected grades far worse than theirs. When I first found the card, I hesitated, thinking maybe I should hide it away, until I realized that such concealment is what the shadow is all about. When I showed it to them, it became my ticket to an easier relationship and a source of more willingness on their part to hear what I had to say.

A client with whom I discussed this issue is able to tell his son that he made straight As. But because those grades have not made up for his lack of confidence, he has driven his son mercilessly, and every conversation about school has been a battle. That is changing because the man is handling the shadow within himself and has less need to unconsciously project his own insecurities onto his son.

Facing Our Shadow

Since our shadow is the unknown part of ourselves, how do we know what it contains? One way is by doing something we don't always like to do, such as noticing the objects of our extreme hate. What we hide inside is like trapped energy that has to go somewhere, so it is projected onto others.

A fifty-six-year-old carpenter named Kenneth was obsessed with hateful feelings at the sight of a man with whom he worked. This was so distracting to him that the feelings interfered with his work even when the man wasn't around. I suggested to Kenneth that when we have an irrational reaction to someone, it is sometimes helpful to ask what we most dislike about the person. That will be our tip-off that we are seeing something of ourselves in the other. But Kenneth said this was not of much help because what he most disliked about his co-worker was the man's nasty, mean attitude, and he himself, in honesty, was not nasty or mean.

I saw myself in Kenneth. I asked him if he ever lost his temper out of nowhere, and he said yes, adding, "It's a crazy thing. I don't know where it comes from, but when it happens, I can snap your head off." I said, "That sounds pretty mean." Kenneth began to recognize the repressed rage beneath his nice guy persona. When he began to focus on that rage, the obsession lost its grip. But lasting gains came only after he paid attention to the positive qualities his fear of rage had suppressed—his ability to take a stand and express his ideas.

Who Fascinates You?

Also, we unconsciously see ourselves in the people we admire. When we are so fascinated by another person that we could watch them express their talent all day, that's a sign that we are dealing with our unlived lives. Though we would deny it, somehow we have what they have, and when possible, we should go out and live what we think exists in the other person. When we don't do that, it can cause problems in our relationships because "the other" is seen as always capable of doing the things we could never do. Rather than flatter the other person, that kind of perfection burdens a person with expectations that can never be met. Relief comes from claiming what is rightfully ours.

Noticing what greatly disturbs or fascinates us in others, then, is our red flag that we are dealing with something unfinished within ourselves. The emotion is so strong that we can't seem to jar loose from it. When it is negative, though we attempt to appear cool, it is not a secure feeling. Taking back what we have disclaimed is sometimes difficult, but when we are at least open to the possibility that our disturbance is from our own shadow, we are well on the way.

When I recognize the signs that tell me I am projecting onto others, even though I have no clue as to what it is, I find it helpful to say, "If what I see in this other person is in any way within me, I want to know what it is." Before long, I begin to feel relief, and I usually get a good idea about what's gnawing at me. It's also helpful to know that taking a good look in the bag can only help me because even the traits I think are negative are potentially creative. But that constructive stage can't be reached as long as the traits are lost in the dark. So the point is not to stop blaming others and start blaming ourselves. We don't blame anyone as we turn our attention to those things within us that are most creative.

Creativity's Shadow

Acceptance of the shadow is increasingly important in this book as we talk about more active ways to create our lives. Every creative step is linked to a necessary shadow, and if we tolerate only perfection, all of our creations will, in time, self-destruct. Opening to the shadow is simply the willingness to face the truth. As we affirm that there is nothing to fear from the truth, we are less defensive, more connected to our surroundings. Relationships are easier, and we are freer to take realistic risks.

Just as ignoring the shadow can make life unruly and confused, acknowledging it can restore the clarity we need to move on. If we accept the unknown as necessary and natural, we will be attentive to shortcomings rather than embarrassed by them, forgiving rather than judgmental. Then when courageously faced, even parts of us that appear to be destructive can be transformed. Uncontrolled anger can lead us to assertiveness. Envy can show us what we want. Days in the dumps can help us reorder our lives. When we stop demanding that life be ultra smooth, we can take disappointments in stride. We won't jump to so many dreadful conclusions, and we'll work with, rather than against, the things that disrupt our plans. With less to hide, there is more to laugh at, especially in ourselves, another sure sign that we are making friends with our shadow.

Practice this—

1. Think of a friend, acquaintance, or public figure that you find very disturbing. The person is so troubling to you that you can't stop thinking about him or about what he does. You are haunted by the person's coldness, self-centeredness, or insensitivity. Reminding yourself that you can only gain by bringing your own shadow to light, begin to say, "If there is a part of me that resembles that person, I want to know what it is." Don't try to figure out what your internal trigger may be. Simply notice what you feel and what comes to mind as you calmly and sincerely say the words over the next few days. You might keep a short record of what emerges in your journal. As ideas come up, ask yourself what positive traits you may have stowed out of sight by disclaiming what you thought was a destructive trait.

2. Think of a friend, acquaintance, or public figure that you admire so much that the person fascinates you. You are enthralled by the way the person conducts business, hits a ball, or communicates with others. Say to yourself, "If I am like that person in any way, I want to know how." At first, rather than try to change your behavior, just continue to ask the question. In time, begin to try on some new behavior. If the new behavior doesn't feel just right, stick with it as you would a new pair of shoes that may be just right for you when broken in.

CHAPTER 10

Our Cast of Characters

Raymond, a lawyer, was in turmoil because of a lawsuit brought against him that threatened his practice. He was plagued by an assortment of feelings to which he did not easily admit, including anger, fear, and embarrassment. All his life, he had been single-minded. When problems arose, he easily cut to a solution. Now he wobbled, and every effort to free himself of confusion birthed more perplexity. His resolve to remain clear was short-lived, and he repeatedly found his mind fragmented and muddy. Friends suggested that he go to a cabin in the woods, write in his journal, and let the forest quiet his mind. A recovering workaholic, he enjoyed the slower pace, found walks in the woods a salve, and felt that at last his thoughts were coming from a deeper place, the hub of his real values. But while looking inside himself felt right, it was not the eye-opener he had hoped for. To his dismay, at times it was as if he heard as much disagreement coming from inside as from outside.

The Raymond in All of Us

Doesn't Raymond's experience sound familiar? Despite our attempts to be decisive, we experience conflict. We want to move on, and we want to stay put. Duty calls, and we want to play. In the morning we are high, by noon depressed. Our visions and desires are mixed with guilt and caution. And too often, in spite of the serenity of nature or the peace of a chapel, we still find ourselves bewildered.

We're More Interesting than We Think

When Raymond asked what I thought of his predicament, I gave him a book written by psychologists Hal Stone and Sidra Winkelman, *Embracing Our Selves*. The book says that we are much more interesting than the single-minded persons we struggle to be. Rather than a solitary personality, it suggests that we are more like a cast of characters that represent many different points of view, feelings, attitudes, and moods. The characters inside us are at once adults and children, men and women, wise people and fools. They are the mother and father in us, the doctor and patient, the hermit and partygoer, the saint and ruthless criminal. Our cast can give us information, shed light on unexplained fears, and help us do what we can't do by ourselves. Remembering his childhood, Jung made an appealing statement: "The small boy is still around and possesses a creative spirit which I lack."

If we listen to everyone in our life drama, even the ones we prefer not to claim, they all have something to contribute. While no one of them has all the answers, attention to what each has to say gives us glimpses of the whole truth. Disregard for them leaves us incomplete, and that incompletion breeds anxiety, depression, and even physical symptoms. As we said in the last chapter, when we do not accept a part of ourselves, it is locked away in our shadow. Loving each part means giving each part respectful attention, seeking to understand what it wants and needs without turning our lives over to any one of them. To illustrate, let's get back to Raymond.

Giving All Our Parts a Fair Hearing

Raymond said that part of him wanted to chew his opponents up at any cost. Later in the conversation, he said that part of him wanted to let the matter go, that it wasn't worth the stress. Then after a few minutes, he said that part of him wanted to give up law altogether. When I pointed out how often he used the phrase "part of me," he said, "Oh, yes, and it's very confusing when I do that." I suggested that when he found himself saying "part of me," he imagine he is speaking for an actual person living inside who might have something important to say. He was to stop at that point and give the person his full attention. He agreed to some homework. For the next week, he would listen to each of those parts and write what he heard. He was to listen to one part at a time and not let the others interfere. Each would have his or her time. Also I suggested that regardless of what he heard, he not come to any conclusions about doing anything differently.

The following week he told me that he was surprised at the strength of those voices, especially the one that wanted to chew his opponents up. At first, this concerned him because it was so unlike the compliant and submissive person he had always been. But there was decisiveness in that character and an ease of speech that he found enlivening. In his journal, he worked with all of these characters for several weeks, and, instead of the casual remark, "Part of me says," he would allow each part to speak freely and in detail. As he became more familiar with these aspects of himself, to his surprise, he often found that the ones he most resisted had something constructive to offer.

For instance, behind the part that wanted to chew his opponents up was a person who could be justifiably angry, clear, and direct. He then became more familiar with a courageous part of himself, which, for most of his life, he had held in check due to memories of a violent father. Before that discovery, when disagreements were accompanied by anger, those memories automatically canceled or diluted his feelings. By giving all of his parts a hearing, he found that assertiveness could keep company with fairness and sensitivity. He now not only listens to what his parts have to say but he dialogues with them, something we will talk about in the following chapter.

Against Our Grain

Raymond learned something that is very difficult in our culture: to accept his many-sidedness rather than fight against it. To many people, this is as distant, and perhaps as heretical, as the notion of the many gods of the Greeks. But in his book *Care of the Soul,* psychologist Thomas Moore suggests that emotionally we emulate the polytheism of the Greeks who had many different gods and recognized the contribution of each.

Jung gives us another reason that we are slow to accept our cast of characters. He observed that people have always been frightened of emotions getting out of hand and have run a tight ship around their inner parts, guarding against anything but a single point of view. He said, "All mankind's strivings have therefore been directed toward the consolidation of consciousness." In other words, to keep an acceptable front, the human race has always striven for the same singlemindedness for which Raymond so desperately aimed. Individually, like him, we have our unconscious reasons for disallowing parts of ourselves to participate in our lives. We should not be surprised, then, if we are slow to accept ourselves as many-sided.

How to Allow Democracy in Our Souls

Given our resistance to accepting all of our parts, how do we go about allowing more democracy within ourselves? The first, and perhaps most important step, is to acknowledge as natural that the characters inside often have a way of their own against which reason can be of no help. How often, in spite of determination to act differently or do the right thing, does something foil our resolutions, disturb our sleep in the night, and get us into arguments and scraps? When we admit that these feeling are not signs of imbalance or irresponsibility, we are conceding that in addition to our prized ego, there are many other "people" within ourselves to be reckoned with. We then move from brawls in the soul to negotiation.

If we acknowledge the autonomy of our cast of characters, some perplexing issues become understandable, such as why we break firm resolutions, fall prey to addictions, or so easily jump on the worry-go-round. If we are free of blame, it's easier to turn the spotlight inside. Instead of asking, "What's wrong with me now?" we can ask, "Who inside have I neglected?" We can shift from "Who out there is doing this to me, and who can make it right?" to "Who within me is questioning, crying, hurting, and what does he or she need?"

Nothing Mystical Here

Remember that thinking of yourself as a cast of characters is only a way to help us manage what is already obvious. When we say, "I'm just not myself today," we are saying, "Someone else has taken over." When we solve a problem by imagining how a bolder or gentler person than ourselves would handle it, we are permitting a normally silent part of ourselves to speak. Being emotionally moved by a book or movie is a tip-off that we are in the presence of one or more of our cast of characters. These experiences show us that while we are not dealing with real people, we are dealing with realities. When we do that, we are in good company because allowing these fantasies is not dissimilar to the way Einstein made his discoveries. The theory of relativity came from his imagining himself riding on a light beam at the speed of light. He didn't actually ride on a beam of light, but by imagining the scenario, he unearthed a reality that changed our world view.

The Zorro Within Me

Like Einstein, we may need to recapture a bit of our imaginative childhood spirit. Recently I saw a remake of the movie *The Mask of Zorro* to see if it would rekindle some of the old fire it stirred within me at age ten. When, as a child, I emerged squinting in the sun after the darkness of the theatre on Saturday morning, it was as if a new personality awakened in me. At home, donning my mask and cape, I *was* Zorro, flipping and flying in the vacant lots of Houston's Third Ward. A priest friend of our family was so amused at my skinny frame wielding the sword of justice that he nicknamed me Zorro. Neither he nor my parents were concerned that I was delusional, and who knows how much the black and white figure on the screen drew out of me the virtues of courage and service. Our friend called me Zorro until I was an adult when I then became to him just Felix. I took his lead, as we all do, put away my sword, and stopped dreaming. Everyone must grow up, but too often when we do that, we cease to play. We then pay less attention to how movies and literature move us and more attention to whether they are a box office smash, politically correct, or fit our ego's vision of whom we are supposed to be. Stripped of imagination, our cast of characters becomes a one-person show.

Dr. Jung Playing on the Ground

How interesting that one of the most helpful tools for understanding ourselves was found when Jung, with much resistance because he was a scientist and physician, followed an impulse to become a child again and build an outdoor village of cottages and castles with stones and materials he gathered from the lake's shore. Every afternoon found him on his hands and knees building and playing, and although it was painfully humiliating, it released a stream of important fantasies that he wrote down. Continuing in that playful spirit led him to the discovery of what he called archetypes, sometimes called sub-personalities, or as we are calling them in this chapter, our cast of characters. I tell the story of Jung's experience as we approach the next chapter so that we might practice what it suggests playfully, openly and imaginatively as a way of getting to know our cast of characters.

Practice this—

This chapter explains why we don't always have direct charge over the way we feel or act. Examples: We try to think kindly about someone yet we can't shake the urge to clobber the person. Or we muster all possible willpower to change a habit that honestly seems simple enough, like be on time for work, and we don't succeed. Carry a notepad and jot down when this happens to you. When you are alone, choose one of these experiences and imagine that while you want to feel a certain way or do a certain thing, it feels like there is someone else inside you who feels differently.

Instead of putting that person down or trying to get rid of him or her as you normally do, tell the person you want to understand who they are. Imagine you are that person, and write what you feel and need. Play with the idea, giving your imagination free reign as you get in touch with feelings and needs. Write thoughts and feelings without censorship until you feel you are getting in touch with something you were not aware of, some hidden wish, some need, some feeling you normally keep under wraps.
This exercise is often revealing and helps you know what to do next. The following chapter can take you even farther.

CHAPTER 11

Chatting with Our Cast

Despite Cynthia's strong willpower, she found herself buried under work. Unpaid bills, boxes of recycling, stacks of paper overwhelmed her. Now, she sat with Jean discussing the problem in partial shade at her patio table. Cynthia was dressed for work. Jean wore shorts, a halter, sandals, and a floppy beach hat.

Cynthia: I've been told that you may be able to help me with my procrastination.

Jean: I'd be happy to help if I can.

Cynthia: I'm new at this. One of the guidelines for a good dialogue, though, is that we try to understand each other.

Jean: (No answer. She is gazing up into a tree watching a bird bringing twigs to a nest.) Oh, I'm sorry dear. What was that?

Cynthia: Why don't you pay attention?

Jean: I'm really sorry. I promise I'll try to be attentive.

Cynthia: Another one of the guidelines is that we keep talking and not judge each other. Why don't we begin with you telling me something about yourself?

Jean: Well, I like to relax and have fun. I love being here right now on this patio. If you weren't here, I'd just watch the trees sway and track the progress of that robin.

Cynthia: (Cynthia felt she was talking to someone she used to know.) I know the feeling. I used to live like that. But, you know, a family gives you reason to grow up.

Jean: Grow up. Does growing up mean you stop having fun, stop relaxing?

Cynthia: Well, not altogether. You have to hit a balance.

Jean: Oh, and have you done that? Have you balanced work and play?

Cynthia: (Long pause)

Jean: That room you set aside upstairs for rest and reflection—when did you last enter it?

Cynthia: But you know how busy I am.

Jean: Honey, pardon my French, but bullshit. You have time. Not all day. But you often have fifteen minutes. You could even find an hour. But you're determined to work your little fingers to the bone. And that's why when you set your jaw to go after the next project, I tell you to put it off. Not forget it because you have to do it. Just put it off.

Cynthia: So you're the one behind my procrastination.

Jean: Not entirely. Both of us are. But I take responsibility for starting it. I love to play, so how do you think I feel when I'm totally deprived of playing? You wear me out. I'm tired and resentful.

Cynthia: That's exactly the way I feel. And I sometimes feel like I'm running circles—making no progress at all.

Jean: And I'm frustrated because I want to relax, to read, to work on the computer, and you're so busy that I can't. So every chance I get, I try to slow you down.

Cynthia: But what can I do about it? There's my job, car pool, dinner, the choir, the kids. I can't neglect those things.

Jean: Look, I'm willing to compromise. Give me a reasonable amount of time, and I won't bother you any more.

Cynthia: Maybe I can start by using that room upstairs for a few minutes a day.

Jean: Yes, Yes, Yes! Good start.

The Miracle of Dialogue

The conversation Cynthia had with Jean, together with similar talks, pulled her from the dead center of a quandary and helped her balance work and leisure. And it all took place in her imagination while writing in her journal. Past attempts to solve the problem rationally were unsuccessful because they amounted to warfare. Those efforts simply aimed toward stamping the procrastinator out. When repeated tries took her around the same circle of shame, she wondered what was wrong with her. She would ask herself, "Am I really that lazy, that weak?"

Jung said something about resolving personal puzzles that sounds strange to our rational minds. He said that if we accept tension within ourselves long enough, allowing the opposites to exist side by side without our pushing, we move to a new level of understanding. The conversation Cynthia had on her patio was her way of doing that. She and Jean, the fun-loving part of herself, did not fight or argue. They didn't use their usual defenses of pointing out each other's faults. This kind of exchange is called a dialogue, and from it something new emerges, a new idea, a new insight, a new understanding. That's why theologian Reuel Howe's book on communication is called *The Miracle of Dialogue*.

A Non-Surgical Approach

Allowing divergent views to co-exist and interact inside ourselves long enough to hatch a new product is the heart of creativity. This approach is quite different from the one we often use: "I shouldn't feel this," "I should know better," "Men don't feel that way," "My mother wouldn't be this confused." We often take what Hal Stone and Sidra Winkelman call in their book *Embracing Our Selves,* a surgical approach. We pronounce feelings like hesitancy, envy, and depression as wrong and attempt to cut them out. Because the traits live on in our unconscious, we generate more tension because of the inevitable war that continues within.

When we use the non-surgical approach of dialogue, we make a deal with part of ourselves: "Let's talk. I'll listen to you, and you listen to me. We'll not call each other stupid, irresponsible, or crazy. We will simply listen and give honest responses, not to belittle, but to add some clarity to the mystery before us. We can get to the bottom of this."

A Chat Room in Our Minds

We should give talks with our inner figures the respect and attention we give conversations with other people. When a meeting is important enough, we avoid distractions by closing the door or finding a quiet environment. When you dialogue with one of your cast, abide by the same guidelines and do so in privacy where you can minimize distractions.

However, you may be surprised at what follows when you have a brief encounter with an inner figure when the setting is not so structured.

I've had such a dialogue while driving my car, and, of course, without writing. These kinds of chats can warm us up to longer dialogues.

The right atmosphere, then, paves the way for a good dialogue. And since the ego favors talking over listening, a bit of preparation can put us in the proper frame of mind. Here is Clara's dialogue and a description of her preparation for it.

My Mother, My Self

Clara sat in her study behind closed doors. I had suggested she begin with something I learned from psychologist Ira Progoff. He suggests that we write a short statement of what we are feeling and dealing with. This is what she wrote: "Recently my mother, Maude, had a nervous breakdown and yelled at me. Her yelling brought back disturbing memories that made me question her love." Taking time to condense our words into such a brief statement can help us zero in on our main concern.

Next Clara closed her eyes, relaxed, and imagined her mother was sitting across from her. She said slowly to herself, "I want to know. I want to see." She then imagined she was her mother looking back at herself and said, "I want to know. I want to see." While imagining she was her mother, she allowed her mother to speak her own history. As images arose her "mother" spoke:

"I remember poverty, drunkenness, bitterness. I remember marrying during the Depression and having four children in quick succession. I remember caring for my mother-in-law after her stroke, and how my father forbade me to become a nurse. I remember losing my husband and my son within fifteen months of each other, and how the addition of by-pass surgery overwhelmed me with grief. I remember the fear of living and the fear of dying."

Clara then began to write non-stop, speaking honestly for both sides.

Clara: I've never really allowed myself to say this, but I didn't feel your love growing up.

Maude: I don't understand. I did love you and still do.

Clara: You withheld your love.

Maude: I never wanted to do that. What gave you that impression? I did all I could for you.

Clara: When I saw you cuddle with Leah [Clara's daughter] when she was small, I wondered why you never did that with me.

Maude: I thought I did. You don't remember my doing that at all? Of course you don't. I probably didn't do much of it because I can't remember much of anything except housework and taking care of your grandmother.

Clara: And what about all those negative comments about the way I looked?

Maude: I wanted you to look good so your grandmother and her daughter wouldn't laugh at me if you were messy, which you always were. The two of them criticized me a lot, and it was hard to meet their standards.

Clara: Why did all that seem to change when I was eighteen and got a car?

Maude: I loved it when you got a car. Not only were you older, but we could spend more time together because you could take me places.

Clara: You liked being with me. But you never said it.

Maude: I thought you knew. Maybe I shouldn't assume so much.

Getting Acquainted with Yourself

Clara did not begin with the intention to change her mother, to understand her, or to find the words to use in future conversations with her. Although all of these could be by-products of the dialogue, the main goal is that we meet ourselves.

Because Clara was open to the idea that whoever or whatever we talk to in a dialogue is a reflection of ourselves, Maude's last statement was revealing: "Maybe I shouldn't assume so much." As she read over the whole script, noticing which phrases seemed to talk loudest, which ones seemed disturbing, or appealing, that phrase, "Maybe I shouldn't assume so much," jumped out. She wasn't certain how, but it fit. In time, she began to notice a certain guardedness in herself that, before, was easier to see in her mother. As she practiced being more open and affectionate with others, she knew she was on the right track because it felt so right.

On Speaking Terms with All of Our Cast

Anything that captures our interest or demands our attention, such as a hobby, a career, or a duty, can turn into an aspect of ourselves with its own personality. To the extent that that "person" is hidden, we experience conflict or uncertainty. By getting to know those aspects of ourselves by actually dialoguing with, for instance, photography, engineering, or parenthood, we can discover hidden values and a wellspring of passion. Likewise, a good conversation with our bodies, or parts of our bodies, can clarify health issues, shed light on addictions, or encourage peace with our mortality.

Because talking with a project seems obscure, I'll demonstrate it with a dialogue I had with photography some years ago. Long before I wrote this dialogue, I had heard about the process but didn't really use it. It was too irrational a game for me, and I found the spontaneity difficult. I was able to have the following conversation only after I decided to adopt a serious but playful attitude.

Talking to Photography

I started with this summation: "With the help of a friend, I spent six months building a darkroom. After using the room a couple of times, I entered it only to dust. It's been a year, and I wonder what's was going on."

When I reached the stage of allowing photography to speak its history, this is what came out:

I remember when I first came into your life. I see you watching your older brothers and sister developing pictures in the semidarkness of the kitchen, and your fascination as the black and white images magically appeared. I remember when you got your own Brownie camera and a small developing kit, and the hours you sweated in the closet beneath the stairs of your house. I remember the photography club in your high school that you never joined.

I remember when you spotted that fifty-dollar Kodak enlarger in a shop window in downtown Houston, how you drooled and wondered how to get that much money. I remember you thinking fleetingly of being a photographer, but crossing the thought out because of your failing math grades. Did you assume you could never figure out those numbers on the camera? I remember, except for brief dabbling, seeing you only in your dreams until you were thirty-three. I remember your first thirty-five milli-meter camera, a Christmas gift from your wife, and the delight of taking the kind of pictures you always wanted to take. I remember the make-shift darkroom in the utility room and the decision to go for the works.

Me: Well, let's see what comes of this. I really feel silly talking to you, but I want to give the process a chance. I'd like to know some-thing about who I'm talking to. Just who are you anyway?

Photography: Your urge to be artistic, creative, and to seek after beauty. Someone who thought he was given freedom and was then let down.

Me: What do you mean by that?

Photography: When you got that new camera, I was so glad that you were at last going to set me free, that you would wel-come me into your life. I loved that and felt, "God, finally a chance to breath." I've been suffocating in the dungeons of your soul.

Me: I guess that's why it felt so good to me. I loved capturing what I only saw in passing but which the camera could freeze. That was fun. And it was fun manipulating the images in the darkroom.

Photography: But was it always fun? Was it really fun when you stayed up until three in the morning working on one print?

Me: Yes, it was. It turned into work I suppose, but when I finished, it was worth it.

Photography: Was it? Then why did you stop doing it?

Me: I didn't want it to be that much work all the time. And it would have been work all the time if every time I went into the room, I'd go for something I could hang on the wall with pride.

Photography: You know, I don't know if I'm the guy you need to be talking to. We don't have much unfinished business. But you and the person who is so demanding of perfection might well profit from a little chat. Get clear with him, and you might be able to approach me with the light heart that I, as an art, require. You're always encouraging people to allow for their own mistakes, but I don't see you tolerating many when we meet. No wonder we don't see much of each other.

Me: Well, I'm glad we had this talk. Guess I better have a chat with Mr. Right.

Lagniappe from a Good Chat

The above dialogue is a good example of *lagniappe*. If you've never been to Louisiana, *lagniappe*, pronounced "lan-yap," means an extra something in good measure. The above dialogue is an example of an inner encounter that didn't completely resolve an issue but left me with *lagniappe*. When I finished, I didn't feel as conflicted. It gave me a good start and guided me, as a dialogue sometimes does, toward the real source of my discomfort, Mr. Right. The conversation unearthed other issues I still find useful, such as, why I didn't join that photography club, why I didn't feel I could raise fifty dollars for something I felt so passionate about, and most importantly, what do I do about those same kinds of issues now?

The Best Lagniappe

I believe written dialogue can help make practical one of the most prevalent, yet elusive, concepts in popular psychology, that we love ourselves. What does that mean and how do you do it? However else you might define love, it is openness to another person. It is being so attentive to another that we draw out their best while honestly sharing ourselves, even when the other person seems antagonistic. People who love each other often say, "Let's talk." Dialogue not only leads to creative solutions but adds warmth to the relationship, and it has the same effect on our relationship with ourselves. We learn to be tolerant and patient when difficulties arise, rather than to crack the whip of judgment over our wayward parts. And wouldn't that be a nice way of life?

Practice this—

1. Pick something you are either very disturbed or elated about that you would like to understand better. It may be a feeling, a decision, or an event in your life. If you can identify a person, such as the engineer in yourself or the workaholic, do so. If you can't yet identify such a person, good starters are: "Who inside me is feeling this? Who is confused? Who is frightened? Who, although I remain in this career, strongly tells me to do something else?" Write until you feel some resolution or for some reason it is time to stop. When you finish, read it over slowly and see if you feel differently about any of it. Repeat the dialogue later if you need to until it tells you something you need to know.

2. Have essentially the same kind of dialogue with a similar subject as suggested in number one but practice a much briefer version without writing. You can actually voice the words or imagine them. See what happens as you practice playfully over time, respecting what comes out even if it seems insignificant. You may want to record it in your journal.

Exhaling

CHAPTER 12

Life Beyond Boulders

I magine our forefathers journeying to a beautiful place when a huge, ugly boulder falls onto their path. They become so preoccupied with removing the boulder that they forget where they are going, and attention to the boulder becomes a way of life. Born into this culture, we think life consists of little more than problems, together with worry and fear of future boulders. As a result, we sometimes find it easier to think about what we don't want than what we do want. This is how it worked in the life of a man I will call Larry.

The Man Who Knew What He Didn't Want

For the first time in his fifty-two years, Larry experienced sleepless nights, his mind riveted on unanswerable questions: How do I pay the mounting bills? How do I get more bids? What do I do about these heart palpitations and fits of anxiety? When I asked him how he wanted things to be, he answered, "I know I don't want them the way they are." If I asked what a successful construction company looked like, he would say, "Well, it doesn't run in the red."

We often find ourselves in Larry's story, fluently talking about what we don't want—how frightened we are, how poor, how sick. Yet the ancient adage has it, "As a man thinketh, so is he." If we continually experience the world around us as a series of problems, we manufacture feelings and behavior that assure us that our conditions remain problematic. So awakening to a morning recitation of "This is going to be one of those horrible days" can create a horrible day.

Harnessing Our Thoughts

Just as "This is going to be one of those horrible days" can fashion a horrible day, the reverse is also true. With this self-evident principle as a springboard, books brim with advice about how to create positively in our lives what Larry created negatively in his, and many people use the advice of those books for a wide range of accomplishments.

Athletes use the principle to improve their form, artists to paint and sculpt, entrepreneurs to build businesses, students to accelerate learning, and patients to improve their health. I like to think of the principle not as a technique but as a way of harnessing what our minds are already unconsciously doing anyway. We may not have been conscious of the images we fed on this morning as we pried our eyes open to meet the day, but they were there. We absorbed those images, and they are largely responsible for what we now feel and do. So it's a good idea to know what those images are and to choose them consciously. Here is how I suggested Larry do that, and you can try it, also.

We Are What We Observe

You are sitting where Larry sat in my office, facing a wall with two closed doors on it. The doors are separated, one to the right of your gaze, the other to the left. On the door to the right is a list of all the things that make you unhappy as well as all the things that could go wrong in your life. On the door to the left is a list of all the things that delight you as well as all the things that could bring you more happiness. Since every thought is accompanied by a mental picture, each item on the list is either a conscious or an unconscious image.

Now, images hold powerful sway over us simply by our paying attention to them. I've almost passed out in movies watching a violent scene. In movies, we are moved to laugh, to cry, and we can be inspired past an emotional block. None of this happens because we enter the theatre saying, "I'm going to try hard to change the way I feel." We simply sit down and attend to what is on the screen, and we are moved.

This point is crucial: As you sit facing the wall with the doors, *you can choose which door you look at.* And whichever one you choose will affect your feelings and, ultimately, your behavior. Some carry it a bit further and theorize that when images take up residence in our minds, they act as a magnet that attracts their likeness.

Larry appreciated this process because as he sat between the doors he was not asked to go further than what he experienced. And that experience was the realization that he could look at one door or the other, and whichever he looked at could determine his future. But what happens when the doors with the images are no longer in front of us?

When the Doors Are Not There

In the absence of neatly divided "good stuff and bad stuff" it's not so easy to choose. But the lists are still there beneath our consciousness, and we are paying attention to one or the other. One of our greatest responsibilities, then, is to be aware of what we are giving our attention to and redirecting our gaze if necessary. Most of the first half of this book was designed to help us know what is important and what is not, what brings fulfillment and what does not. Meditation, writing in our journals, and talking with our cast all help us see what's on which door.

We can make an actual list of those things and read it often. Whenever we read the list, we can edit and prioritize it. A good time to do this is at the beginning and end of the day. We can also practice awareness of which door we are giving our attention to throughout the day and redirecting if we need to.

Refocusing on the Go

At any time, we can notice which door we are focusing on. If we are feeling anxious, depressed, stressed, we are focusing on the kinds of images and thoughts that close our valve. We can then choose to recall the kinds of images and thoughts that help open our sluice and choose those. Larry noticed that for the most part he had been focusing on things that kept his valve closed: his failing construction business, his anxiety, his rising debt. During his session, he decided that when he began to worry, or focus on the things he didn't want, he would turn his attention to what he wanted to feel and experience. I suggested he maintain that second focus until he began to feel good, thereby reopening his valve.

The choice to refocus was difficult for Larry. It was not difficult in itself, no more than it was difficult to turn his attention from one door to the other. It was difficult for Larry because he was at home with negativity, and picking at boulders was his usual behavior. Because of this "addiction" to negativity, he soon knew that consciously choosing images that support his life would take practice.

Worry in Reverse

When Larry returned the next week, he reported that often he had had spurts of encouragement. He began to see that this rather simple maneuver could bring significant change to his life. But he still stared worriedly at the ceiling at three in the morning, still snapped mercilessly at his family, and still had not a clue about what to do with his business. Larry was experiencing the backfiring effect that occurs when we try not to worry. If we try to push something out of our minds, we don't succeed for long before it flies right back at us.

Our minds are not interested in giving up things. Rather, our minds are interested in what gives us fulfillment. It is near impossible to break free of nicotine when someone just thinks about giving up an object of pleasure. We up our chances of success when we focus on what we are moving toward: clear lungs, clean air, more energy, and more life to live. This is worry in reverse because the essence of worry is fixating on things we don't want. Turning our attention to what we do want until we feel good is an exit out of the recurring loop. So rather than try to not think about the dissatisfying door, Larry practiced acknowledging its presence. He began talking about it to himself or writing about it until he felt good. Then he was well on his way. So nothing is more important than knowing where we put our attention, at which altar, if you will, we worship.

Can We Really Know Our Heart's Desire?

The easiest way to know what we want is to notice what we don't want because sitting opposite of what we don't want is our desire for that moment. If I'm bored, I want to be excited. If I don't like my job, I want more interesting work. If I don't like my disorganized drawer of junk, I want the drawer to be organized. If we can't see the opposite of what we want, we can at least start with generalities such as, "I want to be happy. I want to feel good. I want to feel passionate." When we're at a loss to know what we want specifically, generalities shift us to the door of possibilities where it is easier to find the specifics. That's what Nathan did.

Nathan knew he didn't like his job as an insurance salesman, but he didn't know what he would enjoy doing. He began to affirm, "I want to enjoy my job; I want my work to be interesting; I want my work to fit who I am." He did this until he began to feel good about those prospects. As he continued, he got glimmers of himself working with fabrics, and paint colors, and talking to clients about the surroundings in their homes. In time, he finished a degree in interior design, and his vision was realized. This was no magical leap as the change took place over some months. But it would have never happened had he continued to voice only how void he was of passion, how confused and indecisive.

When Desires Are Fuzzy

While Nathan began his quest with generalities, he learned that generalities can harden into specifics. And when the specifics began to appear, it was important to continue voicing them, to mentally try them out. At first, he was hesitant, choking on the words, but as he continued he felt a match to something inside. The picture of himself as an interior designer looked and felt right. With the picture in focus, he felt motivated; when the picture became fuzzy, he felt lethargic again. Mere generalities were no longer enough. He needed a concrete picture and goals. In their book *Higher Creativity,* Willis Harman and Howard Rheingold call our source an idea processor which churns out solutions equivalent to the precision with which we "program" the processor. It's important, then, that we hold as clear a vision as we can of what we want, and being specific will help us do that. But there is always a back and forth motion to the process. We grab onto generalities, move toward specifics, then open out to generalities again.

Taking Our Best Shot

Accepting the need for continual clarification allows us to move toward goals realistically and consistently. We get into trouble when we feel that movement should be without interruption. Recalling the pebble and the canyon, we should not be surprised that we are never perfectly clear about what we want. We are always learning, expanding, changing, and rearranging. Every choice we make is simply our best and most honest shot at who we think we are and what we believe is good for us at a given time.

Some proponents of positive thinking disregard this roundabout way of creating our lives. They lead us to believe that because we know how to make pictures of our dreams, we can at last have our way. This often leads to disillusionment. We ruin the present day by becoming overly preoccupied with future dreams and plans. A more realistic understanding accepts that we will experience stalls and bump into walls along the pathway to becoming who we are meant to be.

When Feelings Boil Up

When an emotional upset brings with it a torrent of feelings, those feelings may require our attention above anything else. The loss of a loved one, falling seriously ill, losing a job—these are crises that knock most of us out of our saddle. So if you are thrown into serious grief, a new vision may not come for some time. During those times, logic and focus recede temporarily into the background while our systems stabilize. We can't refocus if we have lost our lens. On the other hand, if we're late for work or misplace our favorite pen, we must decide how much recovery time we need. Chances are, it's less than we imagine when we give as much attention to the door with possibilities as we can. Even when our parade has been rained on, we can ask, "Given my present state, how do I want this day to go?" If we don't make it a habit to choose positively, we will likely go back to staring at problems as a way of life.

Be Outlandish

As you become more aware of the door of possibilities, you can expect some negative input from one of your cast of characters. It may be the tight-lipped, problem-oriented person who says, "Who are you trying to kid?" Relax, don't pay any attention to him. Admit that for now you are fantasizing, play acting your way into good feelings, and have fun. Say or write anything that gets you there. See how outlandish you can sound no matter how difficult a place you may be in. Say aloud, "I want to feel light, humorous. I want this project to turn out as good for me as it has for others. I want it to go smoothly; I want to move toward its completion with confidence and ease," and on and on, to the point of feeling the difference in your body.

After you do that, you will be in a better position to know what concrete steps you can take to bring your project to completion. Also, if there is work to do, you will be better equipped to do it. Imagine that once you have gotten a clear picture of what you want to happen, you allow unseen forces to work for you.

Like a Washing Machine

Modern technology has introduced the phrase "Set it and forget it." As we choose to think of what we want, we are not trying to figure out how to make anything happen. It's more like setting dials on a washing machine whose internal programming takes the washing through different cycles until the job is done. In the meantime, we mind our own business. We don't open the back to see if the motor is doing its job or manipulate the parts to make it go faster. Esther Hicks uses the similar analogy of driving a car. While driving, we don't try to peek under the hood to make the pistons and belts run as they should.

Most creative acts require that we let go and allow our source to work at its own speed; otherwise, we hinder the process. We will talk about this incubation stage of creativity later. I mention it now to emphasize that when we stop grinding and pushing, things are still happening, things we can't begin to sort or plot. It's also similar to the process we set in motion when we plant a seed. No matter how badly we want to know just what's going on below, no matter how much faster we would like things to go, inserting our wills where they don't belong will gum up the works.

When you feel tight, closed, emotionally shut down, your first order of business, always, before anything else, is to reset the dial.

What's on Our Canvas?

If we write the things that mean most to us, we have something to go back to when we get off track. When an artist awakens in the morning and asks, "Where was I?" he looks to his canvas for the answer. As the artists of our lives, when we awaken and ask what means the most to us, we can look to our canvas, the list in our minds or in our journals. The list is our reference point, our point of contact at any time with our touchstone, our purpose in life.

The list is always temporary because we are always learning more about it. It is our alternative to focusing on boulders and problems. If we are in the habit of doing this, we always have an answer to the question, "What am I creating?"

Practice this—

1. Make a list on the left side of a piece of paper of what you would like to do. Don't include big things only. In addition to the degree you would like to get or the weighty project at work, include a trip to the laundry, cleaning a cabinet, or simply keeping your cool in traffic.

2. Beside each of these write some action that, if you do it, will accomplish what you want or move you in that direction. Whenever you complete one of the things on your list or feel you no longer want it, remove it and replace it with another. If you keep such an ongoing list, when you awaken in the morning or when your mind gets onto the worry track, you can ask, "What was I creating?" and you will have the answer. You can also use the list each day by doing the following.

3. At the beginning of each day, imagine how you want your day to go until you feel joy, confidence, and a sense of hope. Do this when you are alone and undistracted, perhaps while sitting with a cup of coffee, while showering, or driving to work. Don't just think about what you want, but follow Einstein who said that imagination is more important than knowledge. Paint mental pictures and conjure feelings using, in your imagination, as

many senses as you can. See yourself doing well and imagine the satisfaction you will have until you actually begin to feel that emotion in the present. Make images of the finished product, the meeting going as you would like, the project accomplished, the calmness you would like to feel. Don't be surprised or discouraged if the image is not perfectly clear. Think of it as actually painting a picture, which comes into focus over time. Begin with whatever piece of life presents itself and "paint" every day. If you would like to change jobs but are not sure of what kind of work you want, start with whatever you know about the direction you would like to go. Do you see yourself working outside or inside, as part of a team or alone? If you are dissatisfied with a relationship, see yourself relating well, feeling safe, free to give and take. As you let go of the images and move into your day, trust that there is something within you that knows how, with your help, to bring all this to completion. "Set it and forget it."

CHAPTER 13

Moving On

Thomas, twenty-two years old and about to graduate from college, feels blocked and has no idea what to do with his life. I hope this chapter helps him. Lucy, sixty-seven, widowed, has lots of interests but is often bored. I hope this chapter helps her. Joleen, thirty-one and the mother of three, has a reputation for having innovative ideas. She wonders why nothing ever works out for her. I hope this chapter helps her.

Unless You Move

Earlier, we emphasized holding visions of what we want to create and taking concrete steps in that direction. Now we are going to talk about how to effectively take those steps. What a cartoon says, "Unless you move, where you are is where you will always be," seems straightforward enough. But so often we feel like our friends in the opening paragraph, like there is a drag in our systems. While, ideally, the fire of our images takes us toward the completion of what we are creating, unless we commit to act on those images, we stagnate.

Fall in Love

What do you do best? Really best, meaning not only that you get the job done but that you enjoy doing it and the work flows as if you're on a roll. Isn't what you do best the thing that comes from your heart and enthuses you? When you do that, you don't have to think so much about discipline or making time for it. Daniel Goldman, Paul Kaufman, and Michael Ray, in their book *The Creative Spirit,* talk about the special relationship a creative person has with what he creates and says it is as if the person has fallen in love. He is captivated and driven. People who don't share that passion are amazed at where all the motivation comes from: "She is so disciplined to get up at four a.m. to work out!" "He has such will power to practice for hours!"

I heard something like that when in high school I learned to play the piano. The first year I took lessons I didn't have a piano and had to practice after school, stopping to do so on the way home. One of my elementary school teachers who knew of my much-to-be-desired academic record was amazed not only that I practiced that way but that I learned so fast. I believe she thought, "Why didn't he do that in math?" The answer is that there was faulty wiring between math and me. I couldn't fall in love with numbers.

But Where Did It Go?

Research on creativity tells us that we are all creative, have something to say, and can generate original, fresh ideas. Then what's going on if we feel we have nothing to offer? Where are all the ground-breaking ideas? Your talents are kept in the closets of your mind by those rules we referred to earlier. It's not that you have no talent or motivation or passion but that you've been talked out of them.

If you go to your cast of characters, you may not look far before you find the person responsible for your snag. You may discover a timid person who would rather you not stick your neck out. You could find an overly compliant person who says you have no right to do what you are trying to do—chair a meeting, play an instrument, be a good parent. You might meet a character who's obsessed with how difficult things are. Often it is helpful to find out which character you've been listening to so that you can deal with him and get on with your life. However, do that after you've done what I'm going to suggest now, which is, once you have a good idea of your goal, simply begin to move.

Can You Just Do It?

I would have sooner believed I could do brain surgery than write a story before a teacher showed me differently. She didn't do so by teaching me about plot, structure, and character development. She just said, "Write." She told our class to allow ourselves to write trash, to continue to write until the tale had unfolded, and to leave editing until last. I was skeptical but, to my delight, I found that she was right. I could do it. That experience turned my attention to other things in my life that I first study, think about, pray about, and talk to friends about *ad nauseam* before ever making a move. Often when I'm mulling over those considerations, the work spoils in my hands. But when I free myself of that excessive thinking, I am always glad and surprised at what I can do. Two examples from the lives of other people come to mind. The first is humorous; the second more serious. I include them both to illustrate that this principle is useful no matter what we are dealing with.

Starla on the Slopes

Our good friend Starla was the president of a successful company where she had regular staff meetings designed to encourage individual responsibility and initiative. She often told the staff something that, out of context, sounded reckless. But Starla knew to whom she spoke and felt good about giving her employees this motto: "Ready. Fire. Aim." She was telling them not to think so much before doing something. Do it and then think. This is how her philosophy affected the rest of her life.

My wife, Patsy, and I, together with other friends, started a yearly tradition of spring skiing. After a few years, Starla and her husband Larry, both of whom had never skied, joined us for a trip to Winter Park, Colorado. I have delightful memories of Starla learning to ski. Without hesitation, and having had just enough instruction to keep her alive, she took the lift to the top of the bunny slope. While the other beginners looked down the hill with furrowed brows, she pushed off. Within seconds, she fell. She got up, staggered, and fell again. Every time we looked her way, Starla was falling, tumbling, and, laughing. However, each time she descended, there were fewer falls, and within a day, she was comfortable on the beginner slopes, and by the end of the week, she skied the intermediate slopes. Would that I had that healthy, humorous recklessness all the time!

Stephen at His Computer

Stephen, a graphic artist, often heard from friends that his talents were underused. He knew that success rested upon hanging the right shingle in the right place, but he was painfully shy and hesitant.

So, although his artistic skills were unmatched, his cash flow was mediocre. The suggestion to "just do it" didn't make a dent in his negative attitude. He was more willing to try when we settled on this plan.

First, he was to begin a regular practice of calming himself through deep relaxation, and, while relaxed, he was to imagine himself feeling good telling others about what he had to offer. Secondly, he was to commit to taking any action, no matter how small, that would bring him closer to doing that. Thirdly, he was to follow that action with another and another until he felt he was accomplishing what he wanted to do. Fourthly, he was to commit to having a good time while performing those actions. Fifthly, and this was the one that got him to accept the assignment, if he got too anxious, he could stop.

Stepping Out

Stephen began to awaken in the morning by replacing his usually dreaded thoughts of failure with pictures of himself enjoying telling people about his business. Doing this until he felt good about it took practice, but he persisted.

One day, while working at his computer with a stack of beautiful brochures that nobody had seen but him, Stephen took what was for him a leap. He decided to give a handful of the brochures to the secretary of the corporation next door. The next day, he took them to another suite and, to his amazement, he was thanked. After two weeks, a law firm called him about making a website, and he was spurred on further. Over time, Stephen has become more comfortable marketing himself though doing so is still not his favorite thing to do.

When Overwhelmed

Perhaps you feel that your problem is too overwhelming to do what Starla or Stephen did. However, I would suggest that the more overwhelming your situation, the more you need to take action that you see as achievable, and do so repeatedly. Researchers at Stanford University studied the effects of extreme fear on the immune system of a woman who had a debilitating fear of snakes. Shown in the TV series *The Heart of Healing*, Joann was relieved of her phobia in four hours, something that normally takes weeks or months. At the beginning of the study, she could hardly be in the same room with even a picture of a snake.

With the help of a coach, Joann moved one safe step at a time toward an aquarium containing a sizable snake and was able, with a smile, to pick the aquarium up. This is an amazing example of transcending old beliefs through commitment to action. The therapist did not talk about how or when her problem started, but helped her move in the direction she wanted to go. I would never discount the need for knowing how some of our hurtful scripts started, but doing so is not always necessary. Interestingly, blood samples taken from Joann before and after she overcame the phobia showed a twenty-five percent increase in her lymphocytes, immune cells that keep our bodies disease free. Taking action and being proud of it is good for our health.

A Blueprint for Moving On

Creativity often starts with an idea, or a spark of an idea: "I think I would like to…" or "Maybe I could…." Rather than allow those sparks to vanish, you can fuel them with your imagination and by moving in the direction of your vision. Begin by creating an image of what you want that is so vivid that you feel good about it. You bought the land, and you feel great walking on it. You talked to your child, and it is wonderful that things are working well between the two of you. The image, together with the feeling, will act as a fire energizing you toward your goal and inspiring you to do whatever you need to do.

No matter where you are in your project, nothing is more important than you keep that image so clear that you feel good about it, *and* you take the next evident and safe step. If you lose the image, you are out of fuel and need to stop and fill up. Begin again to conjure your vision in your imagination, write about what you want in your journal, or talk to yourself about your project, until you feel good again. From that more open stance, *move*. If you feel stuck, do anything. Pick up the phone; ask a question; walk in the right direction. It makes no difference where you start. If nagging doubts persist, you can address those with some of the listening techniques mentioned in previous chapters.

Good Tip from a Mountaineer

Whenever I get stuck in too much thinking, I read what W.H. Murray, a mountaineer and author, said: "The moment one definitely commits oneself, then providence moves, too. All sorts of things occur to help one that would never otherwise have occurred. A whole stream of events issues from the decision, raising in one's favor all manner of unforeseen incidents and meetings and material assistance, which no man could have dreamed would have come his way."

Practice this—

1. Think of something about which you are at an impasse. Every day for the next week, sit with a pen and paper or at your computer, and write phrases beginning with "I can…." Complete each phrase by writing what you can do to either complete or bring you closer to completing what you want. Write quickly and without much thought, listing any hunch or idea that crosses your mind. When you do this, try to fill up a page or write non-stop for ten minutes. From your list, you should get a few ideas that seem workable. Either do them immediately or set aside a definite time to do one or all of them as soon as possible.

2. Whenever you are thinking of something you would like to have different in your life, do something that will move you toward it.

3. Every day renew the rules:
   a) No step is too small.
   b) It makes no difference where you start.
   c) Have fun.

CHAPTER 14

The Reset Button

Laid off as a manager in an insurance company, Connie escaped the blues by opening a booth in an art show displaying her handcrafted pottery. Coincidentally, she was reading a book on positive thinking and hoped her fate would change. She loaded her apartment with books and tapes that pumped her with hope and posters that reminded her, "Whatever you can imagine, you can have." Her booth practically sold out and that encouraged her to make more pottery that she sold from her house and later from a small shop. By the end of the year, with national consignments, her spirits kicked into high gear.

Connie's Sugar High

Connie was delighted that she could at last take charge rather than be a victim, but in time she deflated. Positive thinking kept her business afloat, but it did not save her house from a flood or her brother from AIDS. She then thought her successes were just accidents and reverted to believing she had no control whatsoever. She told me that her life had certainly felt good for a while only to drop as if from a sugar high.

Making the Ego the Culprit

In her effort to climb out of that hole, Connie attended a lecture based on an Eastern poem that begins, "The Great Way is not difficult for those who have no preferences." The speaker said that desires thwart happiness and set us up for disappointment. She decided to retire her ego, let go of desires and plans, and just wait for her unconscious to move her. While at first relieved, she eventually became listless and depressed, surrounded by piles of uncompleted projects that her unconscious never seemed to get around to doing. Also, try as she might, she couldn't quash her desires.

One day, while browsing the library, she came across the words she had heard in the lecture, but they were translated in a different way. This version read, "The Great Way is not difficult for those who are *unattached* to their preferences." She immediately saw the difference between having no preferences and being unattached to preferences. That difference ignited a new thought: that she could still have desires while not being enslaved by them. In time, the new thought and the experiences that came from living it, unlocked the exit gate from her depression.

Why the Ego Gets Bad Press

Choice is a two-edged sword. On the one hand, it is a great gift moving us toward what's most important. However, as soon as we begin to choose, the ego tends to constrict, seeing no other path than the one it wants. This blindness can cut us off from our source where our true values and purpose reside. We then make choices that don't fit and lose motivation to finish what we set out to do. From such frustrating experiences come popular ego-bashing maxims like "Life is what happens while we are making plans," and "If you want to make God laugh, tell Him your plans."

Connie's more workable attitude came not from giving up desires but from learning to hold her desires with flexibility while she remained open to other possibilities. She began to see that as she stayed mindful of her source, choosing to move about the whole canyon instead of staying cramped in the pebble, detachment took on a positive meaning. It gave her the freedom to allow more of her hidden potential to emerge, opening the tap to her wellspring of ideas, inspirations, and talents. Because I so closely identify with Connie, I have added another maxim to those above, "If you want to ruffle God's feathers, tell Him you have no plans."

Harry Potter or a Mountain Train

Magic seduces us. We would love, as Harry Potter did, to visit a magic shop and find the wand just suited to us. Then with one dazzling flourish, we could materialize our every wish. But creativity is usually a process over time, during which we move through certainty and doubt, like a mountain train passing alternately through tunnels and light. The journey seems to carry us through barren waste before reaching fruition. Creativity is a cycle of starting out, letting go, reevaluating, and starting over. We do the work, leave it alone, evaluate the product, and begin again.

Most artists and inventors go through this cycle several times. Awareness of the cycle is helpful whether we are building a better mousetrap, working through loss, or learning independence. So in addition to holding an inner vision of what we want to create, we also "rest" the ego to allow unseen forces to work, and we do this, if necessary, repeatedly. If you have a low tolerance for "do nothing" time or feel you should get everything right on your first shot, you will find that rest mode difficult. But nature, as well as artists and inventors, gives us a model that can help us be more patient.

Productively Doing Nothing

Eggs incubate, food cooks, and plants germinate over time during which it seems like nothing is happening. I often find that difficult to accept. It partially explains why, in the spring, plants and flowers don't gradually emerge from my garden. One day, there's nothing and the next, there's an instant garden following my trip to the nursery. And I know of other people, more "racehorse" by nature than I am, who are so hell-bent on galloping to the finish that they find advice to rest from what they are doing ridiculous. If you fall into this category, remember the countless stories of important accomplishments that attest to productive "do-nothing" time.

As you practice slowing down, it's a good idea to carry a note pad because the release of tension often unleashes a burst of ideas. If we write them down, we will have them to act on later. But do this only if the ideas come to you spontaneously; otherwise give no thought to your projects and plans. If you think of them at all, just hold a happy vision of them as complete. If pictures of failure pop into your mind, take a deep breath and ask yourself if those pictures are helping you create what you want. If not, change the channel, and go on with what you're doing.

The Test Mode

At some point, this incubation will hatch something—some idea, some product that we will have to decide, possibly by trying it out, whether to keep or start over with what we have learned. Researchers of creativity call this the verification, or test mode, in the creative cycle, and it is crucial. Now that the eggplant is done, how does it taste? Now that the paragraph is written, how does it read? Now that we've talked, how is the relationship with my daughter? Depending on our attitude, the answers can send us off the edge so that we give up or they can spur us on to a more satisfying life.

Like a Jigsaw Puzzle

When we work on a jigsaw puzzle and find a piece we think might fit, we try it out. If the piece doesn't fit, we don't scream, "Oh, God! It doesn't fit! I should never work puzzles!" and throw the puzzle away. But that's what we do when in frustration we declare, "I'm not cut out to be a father, a teacher, a lawyer. I'm so inadequate." When we conclude that we are inadequate, a picture of inadequacy is inserted into our creative mechanism, incubates, and the effects are seen in our lives. We then point to all the negative things "happening" to us as proof of being marked for bad luck and failure. Marilyn Ferguson, in her book *The Aquarian Conspiracy,* says that "If we take the artist-scientist's view toward life, there is no failure. An experiment has results: we learn from it."

Our Greatest Creation

I find Ferguson's statement even more assuring when I reflect that what I am ultimately creating is myself, and that project is never finished. Each experimental choice serves two purposes. It moves me closer to what I immediately want, and secondly, it is an indicator of what fits and does not fit into my life. It brings into focus what means the most to me, thus sharpening the image of who I am. So every external choice resounds internally, signaling me how the patio I'm working on, the friendships I'm cultivating, or the seminar I'm developing, fit into the whole of my life. Seeing the bigger picture helps me to decide whether to keep what I'm considering, change it, or let it go.

Living experimentally includes bold activity followed by visits to our touchstone to ask, "Does this feel right? Does it fit my nature? Does it serve the good of everyone concerned?" Those stops may include renewing our original picture when we lose it, asking what internal rules hold us back, or simply resting from what we are doing to let the muddy waters of our minds clear.

Writing a Book and Something More

I could not have begun this work had I not acknowledged that I may or may not end up with a book, and if I did, it may or may not be published. I half-jokingly say to everyone who expresses an interest in what I am writing, "If no one else reads it, you will." An inner voice tells me that if I want to remain sane and enjoy the writing, I had better really mean that. To the extent that I have meant it, the writing has been lighter, more personal, and playful. Whenever I find myself saying that life will drain from me if the book is not published or not finished by a certain time or does not look a certain way, the writing has turned stilted, academic, and stiff.

Though I began by not setting deadlines, it's been a much longer journey than I thought, and I've written myself in and out of countless jams. When snared in those jams, my demons would ask, "Do you really believe what you're talking about?" And the answer was not always on the tip of my tongue. Often I have had to set the work aside and see how what I was writing about played out in my life. Then the words would come, not only more easily but more concisely and genuinely. The experience of writing experimentally has helped me understand what Matthew Fox meant when he said, "The greatest thing the potter produces is the potter."

The Man Who Named this Chapter

I once counseled a young man who had fallen into near despair over the loss of a love. In tears, he remarked, "I don't know what's wrong with me. I wish I could push the reset button." In a sense, to the extent that we choose to live experimentally, the button is always at hand.

Practice This—

1. Look over this chapter, and in your journal, list two things that—if you began to do differently—would help you be more creative.

2. Find someone in your cast of characters who discourages you from making these changes. For instance, if it is hard for you

to let things incubate, perhaps your parents were hard drivers who led you to believe you should move full steam, stopping for nothing. Make up a character who lives within you, encouraging you to keep moving. Write a dialogue with that person.

3. Write a description of yourself doing the things you listed in number one. Have fun writing the details about how you feel, act, and look, doing those things because they come easily to you.

CHAPTER 15

Ordinary Stuff

One Saturday morning, one of my sons called and asked what I was up to. When I told him I was writing, he said, "Dad, what are you going to do when you finish that book?" I caught from his tone, "Is there life after the book?" I hadn't realized, though he did not live in our house or follow me to work, how obvious it was to him that writing a book had consumed me. His comment wasn't the first hint that I must guard against allowing something that is important to become *all* important. When only extraordinary things are allowed entrance into my life, I miss a lot of living. It's easier to see this tendency in the lives of others.

I once knew an artist named Joshua who lived from art show to art show, whose life between shows was dreary and meaningless. He lived to prepare for the gallery opening when he could busy himself planning the evening and hanging his paintings, alive with justifiable pride. But once the show was over, satisfaction bled off and he felt empty. We repeat his experience when we insist that our life be special, that our friends be dazzling, and that our work be the best.

Flying Too High

There is a term in analytical psychology for what happens when instead of opening to what's outside the pebble and stepping into the canyon, we begin to think we are the canyon. The condition that occurs when our egos ignore their boundaries and take on more than we are capable of doing is called inflation. The Greek myth of Icarus is often used to depict metaphorically the effects of inflation

To release both himself and his son from prison, Icarus' father made each of them wings from wax, warning Icarus not to fly too high because the sun would melt his wings, and he would fall. But Icarus, too intoxicated by his new-found ability to fly, forgot his father's warning and soared so high that the sun did melt his wings, and he fell to the earth. His father did not warn him against flying high but about flying *too* high, trying to escape the earth.

Happiness Under a Neighborhood Bridge

Accepting that we are tethered to earth means that we find value and meaning in the day-to-day events of our lives. We find value in the ordinary when we are really present as we have lunch with a friend, walk the dog, or read a bed-time story to a child. It means living closer to what it was like when we were children, free to live for the day. As children, we didn't weigh the satisfaction or reward we got from simply doing what came next.

One weekend, our grandson Dylan spent the night with us, and he began to get restless. We thought of taking him to the zoo, which required dressing him and packing a lunch. We also considered taking him to see one of his favorite Disney movies, *The Lion King,* playing at the IMAX. Surely, that would hold his attention. We decided to let him show the way. That led him and me for a walk to "the ditch," a steep drainage canal that may as well have been the Mississippi River. As we walked the crest of the slope, Dylan couldn't have been more content, just tossing sticks and rocks into the water. We found ourselves under a bridge where we struck gold, an assortment of rocks and sticks of all sizes. We must have been under those huge beams for over an hour. The simple pleasures are sometimes the best.

Showstoppers

As we grow up, we learn that it's not enough to be where we are—we must be over there, up there, on top of there. To assure a life of high quality and glitzy glamour, we learn to be competitive. We begin to keep score, to compare, to reject anything short of the sensational, and to welcome only what comes rolling our way like a pickup truck commercial, screaming promises to our bored lives.

Last night, I saw a sitcom that reminded me of this. Two brothers joined a spa and found bliss as they were massaged in aromatic oils and wrapped in warm steam. Then they spotted a senator they knew going through a locked door, and they were told he was entering the gold area, a cut above their own silver area. They now wanted to enter the gold area, not because their own level was lacking but because gold offered more. So they signed up for what promised to be better bliss. Life was unrivaled in the gold area, until they saw someone going through yet another door. When the attendant left, they opened this door and were bathed in light that they assumed was an added source of luxury. When their eyes adjusted, though, they found themselves outside the club standing by two large dumpsters.

Where Are We in the Game?

Settling only for show stoppers guarantees discontent because showstoppers are rare. With contentment always over there, we're doomed to exhaust our energy chasing the proverbial carrot. We will enjoy life when we retire, when we graduate, when we get a better position, or perhaps after we put the finishing touches on our self-improvement plan. And the payoff never comes. Psychologist Robert Johnson, in his book *Transformation,* suggests an alternate way. He points out that to be happy is to know how to live what happens, since the word "happiness" is related to the word "happens." That's why he observes, "If you cannot be happy at the prospect of lunch, you are not likely to find happiness anywhere."

Psychiatrist Viktor Frankl's experience in the Nazi concentration camps led him to conclude that we find meaning in the present. The thrust of his therapy, written about in his book *Man's Search for Meaning: An Introduction to Logotherapy*, is in finding meaning. But he said that the question of meaning is rather like asking what the best move on a chessboard is—it depends on where you are in the game.

Just Bake Lasagna

Where are we in the game right now? I ask that question when I get stuck pondering life's imponderables or thinking I won't be happy until I get that new gadget, remodel our house again, or, God forbid, reach enlightenment. Nothing pulls me out of the clouds of abstraction and pegs me to the earth like deciding to just bake lasagna. Not that the new gadget or the house is unimportant. But decisions that require a lot of planning fall more easily into place when I tend to life in the present. If we lose our connection to what gives us joy now, we can toss our search for deeper meaning into the garbage can.

Dottie and Rosie

I am writing this chapter on a bright, cool day by the rippling waters of Lake Conroe, with a fresh cup of coffee at my side. I have just been attacked by Dottie and Rosie. They are kissing me and sloppily licking my ears. The two dogs have been following me around all week trying to get my attention. Their attack is like a call to me, and I imagine them saying, "Play with us. We're what life is about."

While I scrap with Dottie, Rosie licks from my coffee cup—another sign. My deceased mother's name was Rosie, and she loved coffee at three in the afternoon. I've been trying to enjoy writing and not take it so seriously. Today, my two canine friends helped.

Choosing the Ordinary

Joshua, the artist, thought life had meaning only on opening night because as a child, unless he made a tremendous splash, he went unnoticed. Big shows were his ticket to recognition. Once he became aware of this, he altered his thinking. Slowly he came to believe that he is worthwhile even when he is not in the spotlight. With time and practice, he learned to enjoy not only big moments but little ones, like riding his bicycle, eating an ice cream cone, and playing with his cat, whom he now imitates by taking lazy naps. Also, to his surprise, he found that far from making life uninteresting as he feared, respecting the ordinary so enriched him that it became his doorway to a creative fulfillment. He is a better artist because art is not weighted with the full responsibility for his life. He still prizes excellence, loves being an expert, and lives with passion. And he breathes easier knowing he doesn't have to be an excellent, passionate expert every minute of the day.

Dropping Our Mammoth Expectations

Just as we sometimes fall into the same distressing trap as Joshua did, we can follow his lead out. We may not have been imprinted with his script, but we are all vulnerable to the hypnotic spell cast by TV, ads, and movies that appeal to the ego's need to be outstanding. While just being aware of that spell and choosing otherwise brings us a long way, we can expect our journey back to the ordinary to take practice. It becomes easier as we realize how much energy and satisfaction lies right in front of us the more we peel away those big requirements.

The bottom line: we had better learn to love the ordinary, because it is all we have, since everything extraordinary has a way of becoming very ordinary.

Practice this—

> Think about or write in your journal all the things you don't do because they are out of date or because adults don't do them or because you are waiting for something better to come along. Be open to the possibility that if you just taste, you might enjoy. Do it and stick with it for a while, and see if you don't begin to enjoy a part of the world you thought was useless to you or revive interest in things you had discarded.

CHAPTER 16

Detours, Twists, and Turns

If I could rewrite my entire educational curriculum beginning in the first grade, I would sprinkle it with classes on change. Though we crave permanence, change is our ever-present companion. Just as we think things have snapped into place, the balance shifts: we get sick, lose a job, get a divorce. On top of our personal changes, the world challenges us with new ways to eat, work, worship, and play, all too fast to assimilate and too complex to understand. Sometimes change is positive or chosen. We are promoted, move to a new house, or win the lottery. Other times, it is forced upon us. Knowing how to ride with change is so important that it can determine whether or not we become ill.

The Boomerang of Resistance

While change is a sign of life, resistance to change opens the door to problems because when we resist we never live through events to the other side. We simply loop around to face our unfinished business in another form. To resist we anesthetize ourselves with denial: "This is not happening to me." We distract ourselves with activity: "I'm too busy to notice." We distance ourselves through withdrawal:

"I knew I shouldn't have tried." In our efforts to toss problems away, they boomerang as fatigue, anger, and depression.

Acorn to Oak

Not everyone is as fortunate as the child who brought an acorn to his father, curious to know what it was. The boy's father partially submerged the acorn in a glass of water on the windowsill so that his son could see it sprout and grow. The child excitedly examined the acorn every day for signs of life, but after a few days his excitement turned to disappointment. The acorn had split, and the boy went to his father with the sad news that it had broken. The father then explained that the acorn's falling apart was the beginning of an oak tree. This explanation gave the boy a head start in dealing with life's changes.

Beyond Pebble Thinking

Often our lives "fall apart" not because of a crisis but because of our reaction to the crisis. When stress kicks "pebble thinking" into high gear, we narrow our view. Focused on the worst, we see no purpose, no possibilities, and no oak trees in the future. With only visions of deprivation to guide us, we hurriedly attempt to paste our cherished view of the world back together or dump our dreams. If we master the lesson the child learned, it is easier to believe that what often appears tragic, if not tampered with, may be the beginning of new life and that there is often an order beyond our grasp. Then an unwanted change could be a turning point instead of a catastrophe.

Such a turning point brings us to new levels of awareness where we are richer for the experience, clearer about who we are and what we are doing. So rather than put our energy into trying to stop change, we need ways to help us through it. Then our experience can be a transformation instead of a temporary adjustment. One way to do this is to frame the experience of change as a transition rather than a breakdown.

Bridges' Bridge

A transition is a bridge of time between an old way of life and the new. While crossing that bridge, we can ask important questions and make internal changes that match our life's purpose. This process is written about in psychologist William Bridge's helpful book, *Transitions: Making Sense of Life's Changes*. He suggests that transitions go through three stages: The Ending Stage, during which we accept the loss; The Neutral Zone Stage, a seemingly dormant time of reorientation; and The New Beginning Stage, when we choose a new direction. Knowing where we are at each stage makes the change more manageable.

—The Ending Stage: Rumblings and Quakes—

Sometimes change comes gradually, giving us time to adjust: the company downsizes but forewarns its workers. Other times, the change may hit like a bombshell, leaving us stunned and confused: during a routine checkup, the doctor tells us we have cancer. Whether sudden or gradual, sought after or not, fear accompanies our most significant changes because with change we step into foreign territory. That fear can plunge us into darkness and cause emotional quakes high on the Richter scale. Bridges explains that because we often identify with what we see crumbling during The Ending Stage, we may feel we are losing our very selves.

When the position we hold, the person we know, or the object we possess is seen as essential to life, endings can be experiences of dying. That's when we are most likely to engage the brakes of resistance. And the adage is true: "Whatever is resisted persists, and whatever we experience we move through." But how do we stay with an experience from which we shrink? One way is to accept and express what we are feeling during the experience. Often for the sake of appearing strong, we masquerade strength and coolness only to find ourselves weaker and more anxious.

To use a crude analogy, it is similar to what would happen if we resist vomiting because we want to be healthy. When we do that, instead of feeling better, we feel worse. Similarly when we deny our sadness, our anger, and our jealousy, these emotions hang around longer and grow in intensity. But when we honor what we feel, emotions loosen their grip and we can more genuinely face the reality that reason says we must.

Suddenly Adrift

Michelle had been the public relations director for an oil firm for fifteen years and was abruptly let go. Under her leadership, the department had been like a family whose members not only worked well together but shared personal bonds. She hadn't realized the extent of the lifeline she had into her work and into the relationships cultured through that work. Then the company was gobbled up by a conglomerate and upper management's behavior switched from applause to execution, leaving Michelle not only adrift but lonely and sad. Words meant to encourage, like "There are other jobs," and "Those new people really don't know you," seemed trite and insensitive. She was blind to everything but the flood of emotions that ran through her. She reached for her journal and began writing the only thing that would come out of her, a hodge-podge of feelings. She first wrote about how she didn't want to write, about how embarrassing the feelings were, and then specifically about her sadness, anger, and rejection. When she felt the grip loosening, she was encouraged and kept writing until she no longer felt possessed. She said it was a relief to be able to say, "Okay, this has really happened. Now what do I do?"

Others reach that point by talking to friends. If you do this, choose someone who can be present to your confusion, tears, even your whining, without inserting their own opinion. Some pray their feelings out, saying to God what they dare not say to anyone else or what normally they might not even say to God. When it looks like things are falling apart, this recognition and expression of feelings helps us gain a footing. Michelle said that while she hadn't arrived, the quake was over, the dust had settled, and she could see a bit better. She had moved into The Neutral Zone.

—The Neutral Zone Stage: A Fertile Desert—

Here you are in a strange indefinable place, described in stories as a desert, a wasteland, or a time of darkness. You may not like it here where the past is gone and the future is not in sight. Yet other cultures recognize this time as potentially productive and arrange for the person in transition to go off by himself to realign. Since our main task during The Neutral Zone Stage is to listen to the threads of meaning that still exist beyond our vision, the emptiness we fear can be regenerative.

I have a friend who was physically and sexually assaulted and left for dead. Much of The Ending Stage for her is a blur because of a temporary amnesia that followed the assault. Susan wonders now if that amnesia was nature's way of buffering a deluge of emotional and physical trauma. The time of falling apart seemed endless and when she reached the threshold of what she now knows to be The Neutral

Zone Stage, she was left with questions that had to be addressed if life was to continue. Not least of those questions was, "Why bother?" With the help of friends, she survived the tormenting months and reached a point of relative stability. At that point, she instinctively knew it was time to go apart, and literally she went to the desert.

Sitting Under the Right Tree

For Susan, who had never ventured without family and friends beyond a radius of fifty miles, traveling a thousand miles to live alone for two weeks at Ghost Ranch in Abiqui, New Mexico, took courage. Before going to Abiqu, she stopped in Santa Fe to visit with a therapist friend and tell him to come after her if he didn't hear from her in two days. In an unsteady state of mind, that connection provided protection and safety.

Susan entered solitude with no plan but to be present to herself and listen. She had no strategy for answering the big questions and no intention of picking the brain of even the most seasoned spiritual director or therapist. She simply wanted to let the waters settle and follow Robert Bly's advice to poets: "If you sit under the right tree long enough, the poem will come." To do this, she walked the quiet grounds, wrote in her journal, and occasionally chatted with others. Even now, Susan can't tell you how she moved from disorientation to reorientation or what inner tools moved the vital questions toward resolution. But, in time, beginning with a trickle of ideas and feelings that grew, she began to affirm that life was worth rebuilding. That assertion remained elusive for months after her return, but when she lost sight of it, she recalled her retreat to the desert. That recollection would signal her to go apart again, if even for an hour, and listen.

Where Is Your Desert?

We speak of The Neutral Zone Stage as a time of emptiness, but it is not. This period may be devoid of what we once had or of what we thought life should be. But our *self* is never any more empty than the murky water which, when still, clarifies and reveals wondrous contents. So while we may not choose the desert as Susan did, what is necessary is that we assume a receptive posture and invite the part of us that's not confused to speak. More time alone can do that for you, and you may be delighted to know what fifteen minutes by yourself will generate. You can do that by getting up earlier in the morning or going to bed later or by locating and using the off button on the television or radio. You will more easily get the cooperation of friends and family if you let them in on what you're doing by simply saying, "I need a few minutes by myself."

We want to know: "Who was I when I lost that position, person, or thing so precious to me? What did the person, thing, or position give me that I feel I no longer have? Who am I now? What means most to me, and what do I want?" When Susan asked those kinds of questions in the past, she was never in a position to really hear the answers. The woman before the assault was an independent, industrious pusher who dreaded idleness more than she dreaded being struck by lightning. That person believed that conscious choices would assure her that things would be exactly as she wished, and she had even taught a course on how to make those choices with clarity.

The woman she saw now was someone who had no promise that she would not fall off the edge of certainty, no matter how conscious she was. She also saw someone who, since childhood, had always longed for something that she could only call spirituality or depth, but it was always out of reach. She knew that if her comeback was to be more than a whitewash of old values, she had to renegotiate these different facets of her life. Her solitude and silence helped her do that. She then turned her attention to what she wanted in light of that negotiation as she entered her New Beginning Stage.

—The New Beginning Stage—

Some New Beginnings seem to just happen with a clear line marking the close of The Neutral Zone Stage. Rodney went through the shock of disintegration after losing his job and a time of incubation that lasted at least eight months. Then with the energy of a horse out of the starting gate, he bought equipment, consulted with a business coach, and looked for space to rent. In two months, his shop was open and a new career was humming.

Charlotte's New Beginning was much more gradual and typical. Her husband of twenty-six years walked out with no explanation, remarried, and left town. She spent two years grieving and reassessing her life. She reached a point where she could step into something new but was hesitant and stayed on the brink. While she felt new energy, her horse was going to take a bit of prodding. Still fearful, she called her brother and told him she wanted a date with the safest person she could think of—him—and emphatically requested, "Take me to dinner and a movie." She did the same with other very good friends with whom there was no chance of intimacy and joked about her plan. Soon she announced to her friends that she was ready for a "real" date. The next year, Charlotte remarried.

Nurture the Sprouts

Leo said that his New Beginning started only when he began to honor his hunches and inklings. His personality favored big ideas that yielded obvious jackpots. But, as often happens after a desert experience, new possibilities present themselves slowly and piecemeal. His friend observed that Leo never had much to do with an idea that wasn't bursting with promise and suggested that when Leo got an idea, no matter how small, he write it down. Leo took the advice and not only did he write small ideas down but talked to friends about them and acted on them. Slowly and steadily, those ideas began to pay off, and he felt dislodged from dead center. Reflecting on his experience, he realizes that the thrust forward would have happened sooner if he had paid more attention to what seemed to be insignificant clues. He told me, "I spent a year cursing little sprouts because they were not big enough."

Our Longing to Get Over It

As we move into and through The New Beginning, our fondest hope is that we can nail life in place once and for all. No more need for transitions. But as surely as there are seasons, there will be more changes and more transitions. The only question is whether we will go through them or resist them. Between the big ones, there will be countless smaller ones. Every time we drop the eggs, get stuck on the freeway, miss the bus, we are faced with a mini-transition of letting go, listening for something new, and choosing to move on. To a creative person, transitions are part of life, to be worked with rather than against. Such a person knows that events powerful enough to stop us in our tracks carry with them the potential to crush or enrich us.

We would do well to remember the street poet who reminds us that we never get over anything. Rather, as we go through events, they make their impression, their message forever imprinted upon us. If, while we go through the experience, we trust and ask what it all means, what it teaches us, and what choices are open to us, we can be richer for it.

I would think this idealistic had I not witnessed its practice in countless clients who have found themselves starting over after a great loss. Some of my best teachers have been cancer patients, their very lives at stake. These people discover a depth of meaning they had not known—more solid relationships, a greater peace, an ordering of values. I can't tell you how they do it, and often, neither can they. What I can tell you is that they are people who trust something other than their old beliefs, who allow that visit to ground zero, listen and then make choices for a better life.

These are real people, who, when The Ending Stage begins, neither invite it nor like it. They cry, express fear, doubt the foundations of their values and faith. But their attitude eventually says, "Maybe there is something I need to let go of, and maybe there is a way to do this if I just hang in there and listen." And when they got inklings of another way, they began to act, decisively, yet experimentally.

Practice this—

1. Think of two or three changes you have experienced in the past. If you were not then aware of change as a transition, how would the transition model have made a difference?

2. If you are going through a transition, what stage are you in? What is the task of that stage? How else can this chapter be of help as you go through your transition?

CHAPTER 17

Full Circle

"We do request that you secure your seatbelts as we begin our descent to La Guardia airport." The voice seems to come from outside a jar I am in. Altitude muffles the sounds of people talking, papers shifting, and engines slowing to a groan.

Ironically as I completed writing the previous chapter on life's detours, twists, and turns, I learned that I had cancer. I then found myself in another kind of jar, frightened and isolated. Fortunately, the news was softened by a sensitive doctor who gave me every reason to hope for a full recovery. The cancer was found early and it was treatable, so it seemed I had pretty good bad news. I have talked to hundreds of people who were not as fortunate as I was to have an early diagnosis, and I've often wondered what keeps them afloat. Those teachers were an immediate source of strength and perspective. But cancer in any form throws most people a curve with which they would prefer not to deal, leaving them in varying degrees of fear and indecision. I was no exception.

Because laparoscopic surgery to remove the prostate was not yet available in Houston, Patsy and I elected to travel to New York's Memorial Sloan-Kettering Hospital, where one of the pioneers of that procedure practiced. After we made the decision, Patsy asked, "What do you think it will be like to make that trip by ourselves?" We both wondered if going away alone would add to an already frightening experience.

We never would know the answer to that question. When we half jokingly asked a couple of friends if they would go with us, they quickly answered yes. A couple of days later, we learned that more people would join us, and by the time we left Houston, twelve friends had decided to make the trip. Our fear lessened considerably and on the flight to New York we felt relaxed and comfortable, surrounded by our friends' support.

Love and Survival

I buckle up thinking of Dr. Dean Ornish speaking about love: "I am not aware of any other factor in medicine—not diet, not smoking, not exercise, not surgery—that has greater impact on our quality of life, incidence of illness, and premature death from all causes." Drawing on clinical studies in his book, *Love and Survival*, Ornish claims that if any new drug had the same impact as love, every doctor in the country would recommend it to their patients.

I began this book saying that it is a sampling of my owner's manual, the things I feel necessary for my proper care and maintenance. As I bring the book to a close, I hope I have implied that care of our individual selves includes caring for others and allowing them to care for us. Our New York trip reminded me that I have never weathered any difficulty of significance alone. Love is a large part of recovery and healing.

Hopefully every practice in the book helps us become more aware of our essential connection to others. I stress this now because what has come to be called "inner work" can carry with it the possibility of being so caught up with what's going on inside our own skin that we lose sight of what's outside. We now know that to miss our essential connection to others is bad for our mental and physical health. It is then to our individual and collective advantage to look for common ground.

But, instead of connecting points that show our unity, our radar too often looks for differences that divide us. Our reconnaissance troops precede us, surveying the other's personality, appearance, and preferences, sorting them into good and bad, right and wrong, acceptable and unacceptable. We use ideologies, beliefs, and class as "proof" that we are too different to live in harmony.

Creating Differences

While driving through the country, a man's car broke down, and he began walking toward a house in the distance. Because the house was very isolated, he concluded that the inhabitants must be unfriendly. As he got closer, he saw chickens and cows that reminded him of his mother's family, all farmers. He had never liked them. When he got close enough to see what kind of car the family drove, he used that to put them in a suspicious category. By the time he reached the front porch and knocked, his mind had collected a bushel of reasons why whoever lived there was hostile. When a lady opened the door and said, "Yes?" he blurted out, "Keep your damn telephone."

Left unquestioned, the ego will play out that same scenario with people in our offices and schools and homes. The ego doesn't just create surface differences; it manufactures deeper divides. Literally it turns our neighbor into "the other." Especially when others wrong us, we want them to be totally wrong, totally corrupt, totally lost, totally unlike us—alien.

Of Monsters and Men

In his biography about Joseph Stalin, the author Simon Sebag Montefiore shows not only Stalin's brutality but his humanity. In an article in the *Houston Chronicle*, Montefiore writes about the uproar that can be expected when an author shows the human side of those we recognize as monsters. We don't want them to be charming, elegant, or intelligent. If we can strip our enemies of every semblance of humanity, they stay on the other side.

When I read that article, I realized why the TV series *The Sopranos* is so disturbing to me. I don't want those people to be good cooks, love the opera, or have heart to heart talks with their children.

Afternoon Coffee in a War Zone

It is three in the afternoon, and, as always at that time, the smell of fresh Folgers™ coffee is in the air. My mother's cousin Andrew has dropped by, and they are sitting across from each other at our red swirled kitchen tabletop. Mom could think outside of some boxes but not the religious one. You don't question anything Father tells you on Sunday or what the nuns say in school. Andrew questions a lot of it and, to his regret, brings some of those questions up this afternoon. A fierce argument ensues, louder, faster, louder, faster. Andrew thinks he will end it by saying, "If Jesus was God, why didn't he come down off that cross?" But my mother quickly shoots back, riddling him, "Because you're crazy, that's why." End of discussion.

And how many times have we said that or thought it? "You're crazy!" And if not crazy, there is something else that keeps "them" on their side of the fence: they don't drive the right car, live in the right neighborhood, hang with the right people, or go to the right church.

Our Optical Illusion

While we persist in creating differences, scientists are beginning to show us a world of unity and interdependence. Many physicists, biologists, and ecologists see interdependence as a basic law of our cosmos. It was Einstein who said that seeing the world as separate pieces instead of as parts of a whole is our optical illusion.

What these scientists are telling us is that our efforts to pull together and support each other help us see what already exists, that we are in this thing of life together. I don't think that they are telling us we are all the same and that we should meld into one indistinguishable mass. In his classic book *No Man is an Island*, Trappist monk Thomas Merton says, "If I cannot distinguish myself from the mass of other men, I will never be able to love and respect other men as I ought." It seems that we have a duty to preserve our uniqueness, our cultural traditions and customs and to offer our differences to create a more beautiful whole.

But science is now telling us, as spiritual teachers have for centuries, that the meaningful whole is already there. They further tell us that we enhance our lives when we recognize our unity and diminish our lives the more we stray from it. But who among us can sustain interest in that in our daily lives?

Narrowing the Gulf

I have been told all my life that I should love my neighbor as myself because my neighbor is myself. But often I face the day thinking of my problems, my duties, my projects. I reach as far outside my skin as my family and those I have designated as the right kind of people. If I extend a kindness to a stranger or someone I've marked as unacceptable, it is with little inner conviction. Walking in another's shoes is threatening—I don't like the challenges I face, the things I have to learn, or the contradictions I have to tease out. The perceived gulf between me and others is too vast. But if my experience helps me narrow that gulf, I'm encouraged to reach across it. An article in our counseling center's newsletter suggested a way to have that experience.

Unexpected Links

When I wrote the article on interdependence for our counselling centers newsletter, I felt it was too theoretical, and I searched for a way for all of us to begin seeing ties to the rest of the world we normally don't see. I decided to suggest something I had been trying in my own life. To do it, you imagine for a full day that you and the world are indeed interdependent, that your good and the good of others are inseparable. Also imagine there aren't as many boundaries or as many secrets as you think because what happens to you happens to everyone. There is then no need to interact with distrust or to build walls between ourselves and others.

Putting Out the Welcome Mat

The first thing I notice when I live with this view of the world is that it feels good. It highlights for me how suspicion and passing everyone through the customs gate of my critical eye saps energy, as does building walls. Dropping suspicions and tearing down walls feels freer, lighter. When I first did it, I surprised myself by looking at people when I passed them, at least momentarily, instead of avoiding their gaze. I even found myself exchanging smiles with others. Elevators held the biggest surprise. While it's difficult to speak to someone I don't know, when I practiced this exercise, people began speaking to me. Apparently those people read a different non-verbal message on my face that said, "You're welcome," rather than "Keep out."

Exchanging the "Keep Out" sign for the "You're Welcome" sign was sometimes harder at home and with my close friends than with others. In addition to taking these people for granted, it's easier to box them into our presuppositions because we've "known" them so long. When I put my imagination to work with my family and close associates as I did with others, I often have the same surprise: "more in common than I thought; less difference than I thought." This realization can be quite dramatic.

Instant Brothers

Once, while eating alone in a cafeteria, an acquaintance carrying his tray asked if he could join me. Surprised, I said, "Sure." I knew the person only casually and thought we had nothing in common, no reason to speak beyond a greeting. As he unfolded his napkin, he said he heard that I had early stage cancer and that I was going to have surgery. I told him he was right. He said that the previous week he had gotten the same diagnosis and was trying to decide what kind of treatment to have. Instantly, we were brothers, talking on a level I wouldn't have imagined.

Driving back to my office, I thought about how quick I am to create differences, and I wondered about what else he and I might have in common of which we were unaware because I already had him sized up. I was familiar enough with him to "know" there was no meeting ground between us and, in fact, that I didn't like him. All of that changed abruptly when I learned that we shared something that made differences insignificant. How much easier not only relationships but life in general would be if we took our interdependence more seriously.

Full Circle

During the New York trip we could not get tickets to any play except *Man of La Mancha*—not our first choice because we'd seen it before. But had we known that the revival of this play would be the experience that it was, we would have made this choice number one. The play told the story that says riches exist beyond what we can see. In no other version of the play was I so moved to feel what the producer Albert Marre said while watching the audience, "They're not just watching a play, they're having a religious experience." This experience moved us, at least temporarily, from the confines of the smaller into the larger Self, and that brings us full circle.

Creating our lives rests upon the openness it takes to broaden our scope from the smaller to the larger Self. That openness allows us to practice a healthy "selfishness" because cut from the same substance, what we do for another we do for ourselves, and vice versa. Knowing that strengthens us for the two tasks we often find daunting: to discover our place in the world, and to help others do the same. In answering that call, it's encouraging to know we share the same zocalo— we are not alone.

Practice this—

Do the practice exercise at the end of the first chapter adding the following suggestions. Imagine that as you step out of the pebble you step into a world that is interconnected and interdependent. Where you think there are enormous differences, there is commonality. Where you believe you have built walls of separation, there are seamless connections. As you seek home and safe harbor through individual customs, geography, religious, and political leanings, none of these arise from your core. You are like the leaves on a tree that are obviously different but share the same sap and life force.

As you step into the canyon, not only are you more resourceful than you think, you are safer than you think and share bonds that neither disagreements nor points of view can erase. Your efforts to maintain and create your life become inseparable from your neighbor's efforts to do the same and to create a better world. Take this fantasy with you throughout the day or night. Calmly refocus on it every time you see or experience something that seems to contradict it, not to deny your experience but rather to open to more possibilities. With practice, the fantasy can bring us closer to reality.

Bibliography

Abrams, Jeremiah and Zweig, Connie. *Meeting the Shadow: The Hidden Power of the Dark Side of Human Nature*. Los Angeles, J. P. Tarcher, 1991.

Achterberg, Jeanne. *Imagery in Healing: Shamanism and Modern Medicine*. New York, New Science Library, Shambhala, 1985.

Benson, Herbert and Klipper, Marian Z. *The Relaxation Response*. New York, Avon Books, 1975.

Bly, Robert A. *A Little Book on the Human Shadow*. Edited by William Booth. San Francisco, Harper & Row, 1988.

Bolen, Jean Shinoda. *The Tao of Psychology: Synchronicity and the Self*. New York, Harper & Row Publishers, Inc., 1982.

Cameron, Julia. *The Artist's Way: A Spiritual Path to Higher Creativity*. Los Angeles, J. P. Tarcher/Perigee, 1992

Campbell, Joseph and Moyers, Bill. *The Power of Myth*. New York, Doubleday, 1988.

Foundation for Inner Peace. *A Course in Miracles*. New York, Viking Adult, 1977.

Fox, Matthew. *Original Blessing*. Santa Fe, New Mexico, Bear & Co., 1983.

Frankl, Viktor. *Man's Search for Meaning*. New York, Simon & Schuster, 1963.

Gallwey, W. Timothy. *The Inner Game of Tennis*. New York, Random House, 1974.

Gendlin, Eugene T. *Focusing*. New York, Bantam Paperback, 1982.

Ghiselin, Brewster. *The Creative Process: Reflections on Invention in the Arts and Sciences*. Berkley, University of California Press, 1952.

Goleman, Daniel, Kaufman, Daniel, and Ray, Michael. *The Creative Spirit:* Companion to the PBS Television Series. New York, Penguin Press, 1992.

Hanh, Thich Nhat. *The Miracle of Mindfulness: A Manual on Meditation*. Boston, Beacon Press, 1975.

Harman, Willis and Rheingold, Howard. *Higher Creativity: Liberating the Unconscious for Breakthrough Insights*. Los Angeles, J. P. Tarcher Inc., 1984.

Hicks, Esther and Hicks, Jerry. *The Law of Attraction*. Carlsbad, California, Hay House, 2006.

Hollis, James. *Swamplands of the Soul: New Life in Dismal Places*. Toronto, Inner City Books, 1996.

Houston, Jean. *The Possible Human: A Course in Extending Your Physical, Mental and Creative Abilities*. Los Angeles, J. P. Tarcher, Inc., 1982.

Jaffe, Aniela, editor. *C. G. Jung: Word and Image*. Bollingen Series XCVII:2. Princeton University Press, 1979.

Johnson, Robert A. *Inner Work: Using Dreams and Active Imagination for Personal Growth*. San Francisco, Harper & Row Publishers, Inc., 1986

Johnson, Robert A. *Transformation: Understanding the Three Levels of Masculine Consciousness*. San Francisco, Harper, 1991.

Jung, C. G. *Modern Man in Search of a Soul*. New York, Harcourt, Brace & World, Inc., 1933.

Jung, C.G. *Memories, Dreams, Reflections*. New York, Random House. 1965.

Jung, C. G. *Man and His Symbols*. ed. Von Franz, Marie-Luise. Garden City, New York, Doubleday & Co., Inc., 1964.

Lienhard, John. *The Engines of Our Ingenuity: An Engineer Looks at Technology and Culture*. New York, Oxford University Press, 2000.

Moore, Thomas. *Care of the Soul*. New York, Harper Collins, 1992.

Ornish, Dean. *Love and Survival, The Scientific Basis for the Healing Power of Intimacy*. New York, Harper Collins, 1998.

Peck, M. Scott. *The Road Less Traveled: A New Psychology of Love, Traditional Values, and Spiritual Growth*. New York, Simon & Schuster, 1978.

Pennebaker, James. *Opening Up: The Healing Power of Expressing Emotion*. New York, Guilford Press, 1997.

Progoff, Ira. *At a Journal Workshop: The Basic Text and Guide for Using the Intensive Journal*. New York, Dialogue House Library, 1975.

Progroff, Ira. *The Death and Rebirth of Psychology*. New York, Julian Press, 1956.

Robinson, John A.T. *Honest to God*. Philadelphia, Westminister Press, 1963

Samuels, Mike and Samuels, Nancy. *Seeing With the Mind's Eye: The History, Techniques and Uses of Visualization*. New York, Random House, 1975.

Sanford, John A. *Healing and Wholeness*. New York, Folis Press, 1977.

Simonton, O.Carl; Matthews-Simonton, Stephanie.; Creighton, James L. *Getting Well Again: A Step-By-Step Buide to Overcoming Cancer for Patients and Their Gamilies*. Los Angeles: J. P. Tarcher, Inc.; New York, Distributed by Martin's Press, 1978.

Storr, Anthony. *Solitude*. New York, Macmillan, Inc. 1988.

Stone, Hal, and Winkelman, Sidra. *Embracing Our Selves: The Voice Dialogue Manual*. Marina del Rey, CA, Devorss & Company. 1985.

Stott, Bill. *Write to the Point: And Feel better About Your Writing*. Garden City, Anchor Press/Double Day, 1984.

Teilhard de Chardin, Pierre. *The Divine Milieu*. New York, Harper & Row Publishers Inc., 1960.

Ueland, Brenda. *If You Want to Write: A Book About Art, Independence, and Spirit*. Saint Paul, Greywolf Press, 1987.

Wasserman, Dale. *Man of LaMancha*, a Musical Play. New York, Dale Publishing Co., Inc., 1966.